LEARN THAI IN 100 DAYS

THE 100% NATURAL METHOD TO FINALLY GET RESULTS WITH THAI!

BEGINNER

NATURA LINGUA

NATURA
LINGUA

LEARN THAI IN 100 DAYS

TABLE OF CONTENTS

WELCOME

Imagine: you're walking around in Bangkok, understanding and speaking Thai naturally. Phrases spontaneously emerge in your mind, and you navigate this new language with ease and fluidity.

That's the goal of this manual.

If you're reading these lines, it's because you wish to master Thai. Whether for work or pleasure, the goal remains the same: to achieve it. The problem lies in the lack of time. Good courses to learn Thai in English are rare, and often, the available methods are complicated or ineffective.

But your motivation is intact! That's why you've tried apps promising wonders in just a few minutes a day. The result? More time spent collecting badges than acquiring real skills in Thai. You've tried traditional textbooks, often too complex and focused on grammar. Perhaps you've even considered classical courses, incompatible with your schedule.

My name is François, and I'm French. I am well acquainted with this situation. A few years ago, I went to do a year of volunteering in Ukraine. To be effective, I had to quickly learn Ukrainian, Russian and English. But most learning resources were either too superficial or too complex.

Even worse, despite my motivation and long hours in front of my screen or immersed in manuals, the results were not forthcoming. I felt frustrated, angry, wondering why language learning seemed so easy for some and so difficult for me.

I was about to give up, thinking I was not cut out for languages.

Then, one evening, I met an English polyglot who spoke 11 languages. Impressed by his linguistic abilities, I asked him for his secret. His answer, as simple as it was unexpected, was that one should not study a language, but live it! One must learn a new language as one learned their mother tongue.

Intrigued, I followed his advice.

After all, I hadn't learned my mother tongue through conjugation tables or collecting badges. No, I learned French by imitating those around me, by communicating with my friends and family. So, I abandoned my textbooks and removed the conjugation tables from the walls of my room.

I started listening to podcasts in English, watching movies in Ukrainian and Russian, and engaging in my first conversations. Forgetting grammar and conjugation, I simply used these languages. The results were quick to come: I increasingly understood daily conversations, with words and phrases naturally coming to mind.

My English friend was right: it worked.

Just as it's more effective to learn to swim by jumping into the water rather than reading a book on swimming, learning a foreign language is done by immersing oneself in the language, practicing conversation, listening, and adapting to the culture and linguistic nuances, rather than limiting oneself to the theoretical study of grammar rules and vocabulary.

This is the approach I propose in this Natura Lingua manual.

From the first lesson, you will fully immerse yourself in Thai. In a few days, or even weeks, you will start to build a lexical foundation and mental mechanisms that will allow you to understand and communicate naturally in most daily situations.

Be aware, Natura Lingua is not a miracle solution. To get results, you will need to follow one lesson a day for 100 days. But if you're ready to make this effort, then anyone can succeed with our method, based directly on the mechanisms that allowed you to learn your mother tongue.

If you've already learned your mother tongue, why couldn't you learn Thai?

สู้ๆ (Soo soo),

François

THE NATURALINGUA METHOD

Natura Lingua offers you a natural and intuitive approach that transforms the language learning experience. Every educational content is meticulously optimized to enable you to acquire a new language up to 10 times faster and more efficiently than traditional methods.

Each Natura Lingua manual is based on four innovative principles that reinvent the way languages are learned.

1. The Funnel Principle

We've rigorously analyzed and filtered hundreds of thousands of words to retain only those that are essential in daily conversations. Thanks to this principle, you quickly develop a high level of understanding without wasting your time on superfluous terms.

2. Contextual Assimilation

Each term is introduced in a natural setting, reflecting common daily interactions. The result? A smooth assimilation of hundreds of terms and expressions, without ever feeling like you're actually studying.

3. Progressive Overload

Each lesson meticulously presents new words while reintroducing those already studied. Thus, day by day, you continuously progress while consolidating what you've learned.

4. <u>Multiple Integrated Revisions</u>

Gone are the days when vocabulary seemed to evaporate from your memory. Our unique method ensures that each term is reintroduced at strategic intervals in subsequent lessons. You revisit each term up to four times, reinforcing its memorization without even realizing it.

The Mechanism

What makes "Natura Lingua" so effective is its natural and gradual learning. Each lesson introduces new words in bold while reusing words from previous lessons. Additionally, each lesson is enriched with a "Grammatical Note" to illuminate key aspects of the language and a "Cultural Note" to avoid faux pas during conversations with natives.

Is It For Me?

If you're looking to speak a new language without getting lost in the intricacies of grammar, this manual is for you. However, if you love complex grammatical rules and endless vocabulary lists, then this manual is not for you.

Integrating the Manual Into Your Daily Life

Create a routine: dedicate a slot each day for your 15-minute lesson. A coffee in hand, your manual open in front of you, and off you go!

NB. I highly recommend downloading the audio that accompanies the lessons. It will greatly enhance your understanding and pronunciation. Using this manual without the audio is like enjoying toast without jam: you're missing the essence.

ADDITIONAL RESOURCES

DOWNLOAD THE RESOURCES ASSOCIATED WITH THIS MANUAL AND GREATLY ENHANCE YOUR CHANCES OF SUCCESS.

Scan this QR code to access them:

SCAN ME

👉 **https://www.natura-lingua.com/download**

• **Optimize your learning with audio:** To significantly improve your language skills, we strongly advise you to download the audio files accompanying this manual. This will enhance your listening comprehension and pronunciation.

• **Enhance your learning with flashcards:** Flashcards are excellent tools for vocabulary memorization. We highly encourage you to use them to maximize your results. Download our set of cards, specially designed for this manual.

• **Join our learning community:** If you're looking to connect with other language enthusiasts through "Natura Lingua", we invite you to join our online group. In this community, you'll have the opportunity to ask questions, find learning partners, and share your progress.

• **Explore more with other Natura Lingua manuals:** If you like this method, note that there are other similar manuals for different languages. Discover our complete collection of manuals to enrich your linguistic learning experience in a natural and progressive way.

We are here to support you in learning the target language. For optimal results, we highly recommend downloading the audio and using the flashcards. These additional resources are designed to further facilitate your journey.

Happy learning!

BEFORE BEGINNING

DEBUNKING MYTHS ABOUT LEARNING THAI

Learning a new language opens doors to understanding a culture at a deeper level, and Thai is no exception. However, many learners are deterred by myths surrounding the complexity and inaccessibility of the Thai language. Let's debunk these myths and shed light on the truth, encouraging a more informed and enthusiastic approach to learning Thai.

Myth 1: Thai is Too Difficult for English Speakers

One of the most pervasive myths is that Thai is exceptionally difficult for English speakers due to its tonal nature and unique script. While it's true that Thai has its challenges, like any language, it's far from impossible to learn. The key lies in consistent practice and exposure. Many learners find that once they overcome the initial hurdle of tones and familiarize themselves with the alphabet, Thai becomes much more manageable. Success stories abound of individuals who embraced these challenges and found joy in the nuances of Thai pronunciation and script.

. . .

Myth 2: You Need to Be Young to Learn Thai

Another common misconception is that language learning is only for the young. Research, however, tells us that adults are fully capable of learning new languages to fluency. What's more, adults often have the advantage of better self-discipline and learning strategies. There are countless stories of people who started learning Thai well into adulthood and achieved remarkable proficiency, proving that age is but a number in the language learning journey.

Myth 3: You Can't Become Fluent Without Living in Thailand

While immersion is undoubtedly beneficial, the digital age has made it possible to immerse oneself in Thai language and culture from anywhere in the world. Online resources, virtual language exchange partners, and Thai media are readily accessible and can provide a rich learning environment. Many learners have reached a high level of fluency through dedicated study and practice, supplemented by short visits or virtual immersion experiences.

Myth 4: Learning Thai is Not Useful

Some believe that learning Thai is not practical due to its limited global use. However, learning any language opens up new perspectives and opportunities. For those interested in

Southeast Asia, knowing Thai can enhance travel experiences, unlock business opportunities, and deepen cultural understanding. The personal and professional benefits of learning Thai extend far beyond simple utility, enriching one's life in unexpected ways.

Myth 5: The Thai Script is Too Complicated to Learn

The Thai script, with its beautiful but unfamiliar characters, can seem daunting at first glance. However, many learners find that with systematic study, the script becomes less intimidating and even enjoyable to learn. The script is logical and phonetic, which can aid in pronunciation and understanding. Stories of learners who initially feared the script but came to appreciate its structure and beauty are not uncommon, serving as inspiration for newcomers.

The true challenge in learning Thai is not in its inherent difficulty but in maintaining consistency and motivation. Like any worthwhile endeavor, learning Thai requires dedication and regular practice. The journey is filled with ups and downs, but the rewards of being able to communicate, understand, and connect with Thai culture are immeasurable.

In conclusion, the myths surrounding the learning of Thai often stem from misconceptions and can be easily debunked with a positive and informed approach. The real stories of those who have successfully learned Thai serve as a testament to the attainable nature of this beautiful language. The key to mastering Thai lies not in overcoming insurmountable linguistic barriers but in embracing the learning process with persistence and an open heart.

WHY LEARNING THAI?

If you're reading this text, it's because you're interested in learning Thai. That's a fantastic choice! Thai is not just a language; it's a gateway to understanding a rich and vibrant culture, its people, and an entirely different way of life. Let's talk about motivation. Learning a new language, especially one as unique as Thai, can be a daunting task. However, the right motivation can transform this journey into one of the most rewarding experiences of your life.

1. Dive into a Rich Culture: Thailand's culture is a tapestry of traditions, festivals, and history. Learning Thai opens up the nuances of this culture in ways that are impossible to grasp through translation alone. Imagine understanding the stories behind the majestic temples, the vibrant festivals, and the everyday life of Thai people.

. . .

2. Enhance Your Travel Experiences: Thailand is known as the Land of Smiles for a reason. Speaking Thai, even just the basics, can significantly enrich your travel experience. It allows you to connect with locals, navigate your way more effectively, and uncover the hidden gems that lie off the beaten path.

3. Boost Your Career Opportunities: In an increasingly globalized world, the ability to speak a second language is a significant asset. Thai is particularly valuable in fields such as tourism, international business, and diplomacy. Your proficiency in Thai could be the unique skill that sets you apart from other candidates.

4. Brain Health: Learning a new language is a fantastic workout for your brain. It improves memory, enhances problem-solving skills, and even delays the onset of dementia. Thai, with its unique script and tonal nature, provides a particularly stimulating challenge.

5. Make New Friends: Language is the key to people's hearts. Speaking Thai allows you to make deep and meaningful connections with Thai speakers. Whether it's in Thailand or in Thai communities around the world, you'll be able to build friendships that could last a lifetime.

. . .

6. Enjoy Thai Entertainment: Thai cinema, television, and music are treasures waiting to be discovered. By learning Thai, you can enjoy these works as they were meant to be experienced, without the barrier of subtitles or translations. It's a way to immerse yourself in the language and culture even when you're not in Thailand.

7. Personal Achievement: The journey of learning Thai is filled with milestones and achievements. Each new word, sentence, and conversation is a step forward. The sense of accomplishment you'll feel as you progress is incredibly motivating and rewarding.

In conclusion, the journey of learning Thai is one that promises not only the acquisition of a new language but a deeper understanding of a fascinating culture, enhanced career opportunities, improved cognitive abilities, new friendships, and so much more. Let this be your call to action: persevere, keep pushing through the challenges, and never give up on your language learning journey. The rewards of speaking Thai are within reach, and they are worth every effort.

THE POLYGLOTS' SECRET

The gift of speaking multiple languages is often seen as a rare talent, reserved for a few exceptional individuals. However, the journeys of Giuseppe Mezzofanti and Kato Lomb, two renowned polyglots, demonstrate that this ability can be accessible to all with the right approach and unwavering determination.

Giuseppe Mezzofanti, a native of Bologna, made history with his incredible ability to learn languages. From his childhood, he showed an extraordinary capacity to absorb and master languages. One story tells how he learned Albanian in just a few days to communicate with a group of refugees. This talent for languages allowed him to become a valuable cultural and religious intermediary, aiding understanding between various nationalities and beliefs. His method, centered on immersion and interaction, paved the way for a more dynamic and engaged approach to language learning.

Kato Lomb, a self-taught Hungarian linguist, defied conventions by learning over 16 languages without formal training. Her passion for reading led her to explore languages through books, immersing herself in novels and texts in their original language. She often shared how each new language learned opened a window to a new culture, enriching her understanding of the world. Her pragmatic approach and love for continual learning proved that the language barrier is not insurmountable.

Learning multiple languages is often seen as an insurmountable mountain, but Mezzofanti and Lomb show that this perception is misleading. Success in polyglotism is not based on innate talent but on an effective method and regular practice. Their example highlights the importance of immersing oneself in the language through reading, listening, and especially, conversing with native speakers.

Language learning opens many doors, both professionally and personally. It enables a better understanding of cultures, fosters empathy and tolerance, and offers diverse career opportunities. Mezzofanti and Lomb both used their linguistic skills to facilitate communication between cultures and enrich their own understanding of the world.

Begin your language learning journey with curiosity and an open mind. Each new language learned is an adventure in itself, an exploration of a new culture and a new way of thinking. Don't be afraid to make mistakes, as they are essential to learning. Remember, the path to polyglotism is gradual and rewarding. As Kato Lomb said, "Language is the only thing worth knowing even poorly."

The journeys of Mezzofanti and Kato Lomb demonstrate that polyglotism is not an inaccessible mystery, but a tangible reality for those who choose to engage with it. Their legacy encourages us to embrace linguistic and cultural diversity, reminding us that, in the quest for language learning, the journey is as important as the destination.

INSTRUCTIONS

THE THAI ALPHABET

The Thai alphabet consists of 44 consonants, 15 vowel symbols combining into at least 28 vowel forms, and 4 diacritical marks used to indicate tones.

44 Consonants

Thai consonants are divided into three tonal classes, which are crucial in determining the tone of a syllable. Here's a comprehensive list of the consonants, noting their tonal class:

Low Class

- ก (g) - k
- ข (k) - kh
- ค (k) - k
- ฆ (kh) - kh
- ง (ng) - ng

- จ (j) - ch
- ฉ (ch) - ch
- ช (ch) - ch
- ซ (s) - s
- ฌ (ch) - ch
- ญ (y) - y
- ฎ (d) - d
- ฏ (t) - t
- ฐ (th) - th
- ฑ (th) - th
- ฒ (th) - th
- ณ (n) - n
- ด (d) - d
- ต (t) - t
- ถ (th) - th
- ท (th) - th
- ธ (th) - th
- น (n) - n
- บ (b) - b
- ป (p) - p
- ผ (ph) - ph
- ฝ (f) - f
- พ (ph) - ph
- ฟ (f) - f
- ภ (ph) - ph
- ม (m) - m
- ย (y) - y
- ร (r) - r
- ล (l) - l
- ว (w) - w
- ศ (s) - s

- ษ (s) - s
- ส (s) - s
- ห (h) - h
- ฬ (l) - l
- อ ('o) - ' (glottal stop)
- ฮ (h) - h

Middle Class

- ค (kh) - k
- ฆ (kh) - kh

High Class

- ข (kh) - k
- ค (kh) - kh

(Some characters may appear in multiple classes depending on specific use and pronunciation.)

28 Vowel Forms

The 28 vowel forms in Thai are combinations of vowel symbols positioned around the consonants to create different sounds. These forms can be before, after, above, below, or around the consonants, adding a unique phonetic richness to the Thai language. Here's a description of the 28 vowel forms, considering their general pronunciation and relative position to the consonant:

- อะ - short a, after the consonant.
- อา - long a, after the consonant.
- เอะ - short e, before the consonant.
- เอ - long e, before the consonant.
- แอะ - short ae, before the consonant.
- แอ - long ae, before the consonant.
- โอะ - short o, before the consonant.
- โอ - long o, before the consonant.
- เอาะ - short o (different combination), before the consonant.
- ออ - long o, after the consonant.
- อัวะ - short ua, after the consonant.
- อัว - long ua, after the consonant.
- เอือะ - short ue (specific combination), before and above the consonant.
- เอือ - long ue, before and above the consonant.
- อิ - short i, above the consonant.
- อี - long i, above the consonant.
- อึ - short ue, above the consonant.
- อือ - long ue, above the consonant.
- อุ - short u, above the consonant.
- อู - long u, above the consonant.
- เอียะ - short ia, before and above the consonant.
- เอีย - long ia, before and above the consonant.
- เอือย - ueai (specific combination), before, above, and after the consonant.
- อัย - ai, after the consonant.
- ไอ - ai, before the consonant.

- เอา - au, before the consonant.
- อำ - am, after the consonant with the vowel symbol am.
- เออะ - short er, before the consonant.

Mastering these forms is essential for correct pronunciation of Thai words, as the sound of each vowel can change significantly depending on its form. Regular practice with audiovisual resources can greatly aid in understanding and correctly using these diverse sounds.

4 Diacritical Marks

Tones in Thai are indicated by the absence or presence of specific marks, in addition to the consonant class and vowel length.

- **ไม่มีเครื่องหมาย** (Mid tone) - No diacritical mark
- อ่ (Mai ek) - Low tone
- อ้ (Mai tho) - Falling tone
- อ๊ (Mai tri) - High tone
- อ๋ (Mai chattawa) - Rising tone

SIMPLE THAI PRONUNCIATION GUIDE FOR ENGLISH BEGINNERS

Welcome to your quick start guide to pronouncing Thai! Thai can seem daunting at first, but with these basic rules and comparisons to English sounds, you'll be on your way to speaking more clearly. Remember, practice makes perfect!

Vowels

Thai vowels can be short or long, which changes the meaning of words. Here's a simplified guide:

- **a** as in "father" (long) / "bat" (short)
- **e** as in "get" (short) / elongate the sound for the long version
- **i** as in "machine" (long) / "bit" (short)
- **o** as in "go" (long) / "not" (short)
- **u** as in "flute" (long) / "put" (short)

Consonants

Thai consonants roughly correspond to English sounds, but there are nuances. Here are some basics:

- **b** as in "bed"
- **d** as in "dog"
- **f** as in "fish"
- **g** as in "go"
- **k** as in "kite" (but with less aspiration)
- **l** as in "love"
- **m** as in "moon"
- **n** as in "no"
- **p** as in "pig" (but with less aspiration)
- **r** rolled slightly, like a soft Spanish "r"
- **s** as in "sun"
- **t** as in "top" (but with less aspiration)
- **w** as in "water"
- **y** as in "yes"

Tones

Thai is a tonal language, meaning the pitch or tone used when saying a word can change its meaning. There are five tones: mid, low, falling, high, and rising. Think of them as musical notes that give meaning to words.

- **Mid tone**: steady, even voice
- **Low tone**: start slightly lower than your normal voice
- **Falling tone**: start high, then drop your voice

- **High tone**: start higher than your normal voice
- **Rising tone**: start lower, then rise your voice

Tips

- **Practice with native speakers**: This is the best way to get the tones right.

- **Listen and repeat**: Use language apps or online videos to hear the pronunciation and practice.

- **Be patient**: Thai is very different from English, so give yourself time to learn and adjust.

Remember, this guide is a simplified starting point. Thai language has its complexities, and mastering pronunciation takes time and practice. Keep listening, practicing, and don't be afraid to make mistakes. Happy learning!

Welcome to the guide on ALA-LC transliteration for Thai! This chapter will introduce you to the American Library Association - Library of Congress system, which is essential for accurately reading and pronouncing Thai using the Latin alphabet. We'll explore key consonants, vowels, and tones, providing you with the foundational skills to tackle Thai script effectively. Let's dive into the details and start your journey into the Thai language!

Consonants

The ALA-LC system translates Thai consonants into Latin script, reflecting their pronunciation. Some key consonants and their transliterations include:

- **k** for ก, similar to 'k' in "skip".
- **kh** for ข, sounding like 'k' in "backhand".
- **ch** for จ, as in "chop".
- **th** for ท, mimicking 't' in "top".
- **d** for ด, like 'd' in "dog".
- **t** for ต, akin to 't' in "stop".
- **b** for บ, as 'b' in "bat".
- **p** for ป, similar to 'p' in "spin".
- **ph** for พ, like 'p' in "pot".
- **m** for ม, as in "mom".
- **y** for ย, sounding like 'y' in "yes".
- **r** for ร, as in "run".
- **l** for ล, like 'l' in "lip".
- **w** for ว, as in "win".
- **s** for ส, sounding like 's' in "son".
- **h** for ห, as 'h' in "hat".

Vowels

Thai vowels are versatile and can appear in different positions relative to their consonants. Key vowel transliterations include:

- **ā** for long 'a' following the consonant, like 'a' in "father".
- **e** for short 'e' before the consonant, as in "bed".
- **ai** for the sound before the consonant, like 'i' in "thigh".
- **ī** for a long 'i' above the consonant, as 'ee' in "see".
- **ū** for a long 'u' above the consonant, like 'oo' in "boot".
- **u** for a short 'u' above the consonant, as in "put".

Tones

The ALA-LC system uses diacritical marks to indicate the tone of a syllable, which is essential for accurate pronunciation:

- **No mark** for the mid tone, which has a steady pitch.
- **(à)** - A grave accent for the low tone, which is lower and steady.
- **(â)** - A circumflex for the falling tone, which starts high and falls.

- **(á)** - An acute accent for the high tone, which is higher and steady.
- **(ǎ)** - A caron for the rising tone, starting mid, rising, and then returning to mid pitch.

HOW TO USE THIS MANUAL

Phase No. 1:

1. Read the text in the language you are learning out loud, while listening to the corresponding audio (to be downloaded).
2. Try to translate the text into English, without consulting the translation.
3. Check with the official translation to complete yours.

This phase facilitates the assimilation of the language structure and vocabulary and reinforces understanding.

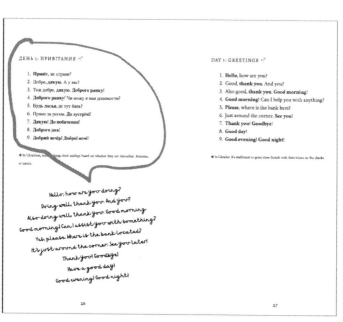

Phase No. 1

Phase No. 2 (starting from lesson No. 7):

1. For each lesson starting from No. 7, first translate the text of that lesson (No. 7, No. 8, etc.) from the target language into English.
2. Then, go back 6 lessons and translate the English version of that lesson's text from English back into the target language, without referring to the original text.
3. Compare your translation with the original text of that lesson and adjust if necessary.
4. Read aloud the original text of that lesson, while listening to the audio.

This phase stimulates the activation of already acquired vocabulary and promotes the improvement of your communication skills.

1. Привіт, як справи?
2. Добре, дякую. А у вас?
3. Теж добре, дякую. Доброго ранку!
4. Доброго ранку! Чи можу я вам допомогти?
5. Будь ласка, де тут банк?
6. Прямо за рогом. До зустрічі!
7. Дякую! До побачення!
8. Доброго дня!
9. Добрий вечір! Доброї ночі!

✦ In Ukrainian, nouns change their endings based on whether they are masculine, feminine or neuter.

Hello, how are you doing?
Doing well, thank you. And you?
Also doing well, thank you. Good morning.
Good morning! Can I assist you with something?
Yes, please. Where is the bank located?
It's just around the corner. See you later!
Thank you! Goodbye!
Have a good day!
Good evening! Good night!

26

1. **Hello**, how are you?
2. Good, **thank you**. And you?
3. Also good, **thank you**. Good morning!
4. **Good morning!** Can I help you with anything?
5. **Please**, where is the bank here?
6. Just around the corner. See you!
7. **Thank you!** Goodbye!
8. Good day!
9. Good evening! Good night!

✦ In Ukraine, it is typical to greet close friends with three kisses on the cheeks.

Привіт, як справи?
Добре, дякую. А у вас?
Теж добре, дякую. Доброго ранку!
Доброго ранку! Чи можу я вам
допомогти?
Будь ласка, де тут банк?
Прямо за рогом. До зустрічі!
Дякую! До побачення!
Доброго дня!
Добрий вечір! Доброї ночі!

27

Phase No. 2

30

Continue in the same way for the following lessons. For example, for lesson No. 8, first translate the text of lesson No. 8 from the target language into English, then translate the text of lesson No. 2 from English back into the target language, and so on.

Additionally, every 10 lessons, a small challenge awaits you to put your knowledge into practice.

Note: Your translations do not need to match the manual texts perfectly, but they should convey a similar meaning. If you are using the paper version of the manual, note your translations directly at the bottom of the text, or else use a separate notebook.

ADDITIONAL RESOURCES

DOWNLOAD THE RESOURCES ASSOCIATED WITH THIS MANUAL AND GREATLY ENHANCE YOUR CHANCES OF SUCCESS.

Scan this QR code to access them:

SCAN ME

☞ **https://www.natura-lingua.com/download**

• **Optimize your learning with audio:** To significantly improve your language skills, we strongly advise you to download the audio files accompanying this manual. This will enhance your listening comprehension and pronunciation.

• **Enhance your learning with flashcards:** Flashcards are excellent tools for vocabulary memorization. We highly encourage you to use them to maximize your results. Download our set of cards, specially designed for this manual.

• **Join our learning community:** If you're looking to connect with other language enthusiasts through "Natura Lingua", we invite you to join our online group. In this community, you'll have the opportunity to ask questions, find learning partners, and share your progress.

• **Explore more with other Natura Lingua manuals:** If you like this method, note that there are other similar manuals for different languages. Discover our complete collection of manuals to enrich your linguistic learning experience in a natural and progressive way.

We are here to support you in learning the target language. For optimal results, we highly recommend downloading the audio and using the flashcards. These additional resources are designed to further facilitate your journey.

Happy learning!

THAI IN 100 DAYS

Check off a box below after completing each lesson. This will aid you in monitoring your progress and maintaining motivation throughout your learning experience.

☒ ☐ ☐ ☐ ☐ ☐ ☐ ☐ ☐ ☐
☐ ☐ ☐ ☐ ☐ ☐ ☐ ☐ ☐ ☐
☐ ☐ ☐ ☐ ☐ ☐ ☐ ☐ ☐ ☐
☐ ☐ ☐ ☐ ☐ ☐ ☐ ☐ ☐ ☐
☐ ☐ ☐ ☐ ☐ ☐ ☐ ☐ ☐ ☐
☐ ☐ ☐ ☐ ☐ ☐ ☐ ☐ ☐ ☐
☐ ☐ ☐ ☐ ☐ ☐ ☐ ☐ ☐ ☐
☐ ☐ ☐ ☐ ☐ ☐ ☐ ☐ ☐ ☐
☐ ☐ ☐ ☐ ☐ ☐ ☐ ☐ ☐ ☐
☐ ☐ ☐ ☐ ☐ ☐ ☐ ☐ ☐ ☐

IMPORTANT NOTES :

1. **The Essentials: Vocabulary and Key Phrases:** In each Natura Lingua lesson, we carefully select the most useful words and expressions relevant to the theme studied. The goal is to familiarize you with the most frequently used constructions in the target language. Sometimes, the general meaning of the texts might seem surprising, but don't worry, it's an essential part of our method. It helps you focus on the practical aspects of the language, thereby accelerating your learning for better understanding and more effective communication.

2. **Translation: As Close to the Original as Possible:** We translate in a way that stays true to the source text, capturing how sentences are structured and ideas are conveyed in the target language. Our goal is not syntactic perfection in English, but rather to give you an authentic insight into the thought process and structure of the language you are learning. This method immerses you in the language, allowing you to gain a more natural and intuitive understanding. Our aim is to help you think and communicate fluently in the learned language, not just understand it. We want to prepare you to use the language practically and confidently in your daily life.

วันที่ 1: การทักทาย

1. **สวัสดี**
2. **สวัสดีตอนบ่าย**
3. **สวัสดีตอนเย็น** คุณสบายดีไหม?
4. ไม่เป็นไร, **ขอบคุณ**
5. **ราตรีสวัสดิ์**
6. **ราตรีสวัสดิ์** เจอกันใหม่
7. **ลาก่อน**

✤ In Thai, nouns do not change form for singular or plural; context tells us the quantity.

1. **Sawasdī**
2. **Sawasdī tawn bàay**
3. **Sawasdī tawn yen** khun sabāy dī māi?
4. Māi bpen rai, **khǭpkhun**
5. **Rātrī sawasdī**
6. **Rātrī sawasdī** jēo kan mài
7. **Lā kòn**

DAY 1: GREETINGS

1. **Hello**
2. **Good afternoon**
3. **Good evening** How are you?
4. I'm fine, **thank you**
5. **Good night**
6. **Good night** See you again
7. **Goodbye**

✤ In Thailand, instead of shaking hands, people greet each other with a "wai," a gesture of placing the palms together near the chest and bowing slightly.

วันที่ 2 : สำนวนที่ใช้บ่อย ✎

1. สวัสดี
2. สวัสดีตอนบ่าย, กรุณา คุณมีเสื้อขนาด เล็ก หรือ ใหญ่?
3. ใช่, ฉันมีทั้งขนาด เล็ก และ ใหญ่.
4. อาจจะ ฉันต้องการขนาด ใหญ่.
5. ตกลง, ขนาด ใหญ่ นะครับ/ค่ะ.
6. ขอโทษครับ/ค่ะ, ฉัน เสียใจ ขนาด ใหญ่ หมดแล้ว.
7. ไม่ มีปัญหา, ฉันจะกลับมาอีกครั้ง.
8. สวัสดีตอนเย็น
9. ลาก่อน

✤ In Thai, the verb does not change form for tense; instead, time words are added to indicate past, present, or future.

1. sawatdī
2. sawatdī tawn bāi, **krunā** khun mī šeŭx k̄hnād **lek reŭx yài?**
3. **chì, chạn mī thạng k̄hnād lek læ yài.**
4. **ājchạ** chạn x̂ngkār k̄hnād **yài.**
5. **toklng,** k̄hnād **yài** ná khrạb/khà.
6. **khǒthǒs khrạb/khà,** chạn **šīa cɪ** k̄hnād **yài** h̄md læw.
7. **mị̀** mī pạyh̄ā, chạn cā klạb mā xīk khrạng.
8. sawatdī tawn yen
9. lā k̀xn

1. Hello
2. Good afternoon, **please** do you have shirts in **small** or **large?**
3. **Yes, I have both small and large**.
4. **Maybe** I will need a **large**.
5. **Okay**, **large** it is.
6. **Sorry**, I am **sorry** but the **large** size is out of stock.
7. **No** problem, I will come back another time.
8. Good evening
9. Goodbye

✤ In Thailand, saying "same same but different" humorously acknowledges minor differences in seemingly identical things, reflecting the Thai approach to flexibility and compromise.

วันที่ 3 : คำศัพท์เกี่ยวกับการแนะนำตัว ✐

1. สวัสดีครับ, **ฉันชื่อ** ปีเตอร์
2. สวัสดีค่ะ, **ฉันชื่อ** สุดา
3. **คุณสบายดีไหม?**
4. **ฉันสบายดี ค่ะ, ขอบคุณ! คุณล่ะ?**
5. **ฉันสบายดี** ครับ
6. **คุณอายุเท่าไหร่?**
7. **ฉันอายุ 25 ปี**
8. อ๋อ, ตกลงค่ะ

✤ In Thai, adjectives come after the noun they describe.

1. sawatdī khrap, **chan chû** phītœ̈r
2. sawatdī kha, **chan chû** sudā
3. **khun sabāi dī māi?**
4. **chan sabāi dī kha, khǫpkhun! khun lề?**
5. **chan sabāi dī** khrap
6. **khun 'āyu thāo rai?**
7. **chan 'āyu 25 pī**
8. 'ò, toklong kha

DAY 3: INTRODUCTION VOCABULARY

1. Hello, **my name is** Peter.
2. Hello, **my name is** Suda.
3. **How are you?**
4. **I'm fine, thank you! And you?**
5. **I'm fine** too.
6. **How old are you?**
7. **I'm 25 years old.**
8. Oh, I see.

❖ In Thailand, it's customary to present gifts with the right hand, symbolizing respect and good intentions.

45

วันที่ 4: ข้อมูลส่วนบุคคล 🪶

1. สวัสดีตอนบ่าย
2. คุณมาจากที่ไหน
3. ฉันมาจากประเทศไทย
4. คุณอยู่ที่ไหน
5. ฉันอยู่ที่กรุงเทพ
6. คุณทำอะไร
7. ฉันเป็นนักเรียน
8. คุณชอบอะไร
9. ฉันชอบดนตรีและกีฬา
10. ยินดีที่ได้พบคุณ
11. ขอให้มีวันที่ดี

✤ In Thai, we don't use a definite article like "the" before nouns when talking about personal information.

1. Sawasdī tǭn bài
2. Khun mā čāk thī nǎi
3. Chǎn mā čāk prathēt Thai
4. Khun yū thī nǎi
5. Chǎn yū thī Krungethēp
6. Khun tham àrai
7. Chǎn bpen nakrīan
8. Khun čhǭp àrai
9. Chǎn čhǭp dontrī læa kīlā
10. Yin dī thī dāi phǭp khun
11. Khǭ hai mī wan thī dī

1. Good afternoon
2. **Where are you from?**
3. **I am from Thailand**
4. **Where do you live?**
5. **I live in Bangkok**
6. **What do you do?**
7. **I am a student**
8. **What do you like?**
9. **I like music and sports**
10. **Nice to meet you**
11. **Have a nice day**

✤ In Thailand, it's common to ask someone's age early in a conversation as a way to show respect and address them properly.

วันที่ 5 : คำกริยาทั่วไป ฉบับที่ 1 ✒

1. สวัสดีครับ คุณ**เข้าใจ**ภาษาไทยไหม
2. ไม่ค่อยครับ แต่**ฉันต้องการ**เรียน
3. **ฉันสามารถ**ช่วยคุณได้
4. ขอบคุณครับ **ฉันอยาก**มีเพื่อนคนไทย
5. **ฉันมี**เวลาว่าง เราสามารถไปดูหนัง
6. ดีมากครับ **ฉันจะ**ไปด้วย
7. **ฉันซื้อ**ตั๋วแล้วนะ
8. ขอบคุณมากครับ **ฉันจะจ่าย**ค่าขนม
9. ยินดีครับ ขอให้มีวันที่ดี

✤ In Thai, there is no indefinite article like "a" or "an" in English; you just use the noun by itself.

1. sawatdī khrap khun **khāo cai** phāsā thai mai
2. mị̀ khǫ̀y khrap tæ̀ **chan tǒngkān** rīan
3. **chan s̄āmārt** chų̌y khun dị̂
4. khxbkhuṇ khrap **chan yàk mī** pheų̀xn khon thai
5. **chan mī** welā wāng rao s̄āmārt pai dū nạng
6. dī māk khrap **chan cà pai** dūay
7. **chan sų̂** tǎw læ̂w ná
8. khxbkhuṇ māk khrap **chan cà cāy** khā khanom
9. yindī khrap khǫ̀ h̄ị̂ mī wan thī̀ dī

1. Hello, do you **understand** Thai?
2. Not really, but **I want to** learn.
3. **I can** help you.
4. Thank you, **I would like to have** a Thai friend.
5. **I have** some free time, we **can** go watch a movie.
6. Great, **I will go** with you.
7. **I have bought** the tickets already.
8. Thank you so much, **I will pay for** the snacks.
9. You're welcome, have a great day.

✤ In Thai, the verb "to eat" (กิน gin) is used not only for food but also to convey the act of consuming drinks, illustrating the language's holistic view on nourishment.

วันที่ 6: เครื่องดื่ม

1. สวัสดีครับ, ฉันต้องการ**เครื่องดื่ม**ครับ.
2. คุณต้องการ**เครื่องดื่ม**อะไรคะ?
3. ฉันต้องการ**น้ำผลไม้**และ**กาแฟ**ครับ.
4. คุณต้องการ**น้ำผลไม้**แบบไหนคะ?
5. ฉันต้องการ**น้ำผลไม้**ส้มครับ.
6. และ**กาแฟ**คุณต้องการร้อนหรือเย็นคะ?
7. ฉันต้องการ**กาแฟ**ร้อนครับ.
8. ได้ค่ะ, รอสักครู่นะคะ.
9. ขอบคุณครับ!

✤ In Thai, to say "I like this drink," you use "ฉันชอบเครื่องดื่มนี้" where "ฉัน" means "I".

1. Sawasdi khrap, chan t̂xngkār **kherụ̌xng deim** khrap.

2. Khun t̂xngkār **kherụ̌xng deim** xarị kha?

3. Chan t̂xngkār **n̂ả phl mị̂** læ **kāfæ** khrap.

4. Khun t̂xngkār **n̂ả phl mị̂** bæb nị kha?

5. Chan t̂xngkār **n̂ả phl mị̂** s̄̂m khrap.

6. Læ **kāfæ** khun t̂xngkār rxxn h̄rụ̄x yen kha?

7. Chan t̂xngkār **kāfæ** rxxn khrap.

8. Dị̂ kha, rx s̄ạk khrū̀ ṇa kha.

9. K̄hxbkhuṇ khrap!

50

1. Hello, I would like **a drink**, please.
2. What kind of **drink** would you like?
3. I would like **juice** and **coffee**, please.
4. What kind of **juice** would you like?
5. I would like **orange juice**, please.
6. And for the **coffee**, would you like it hot or cold?
7. I would like **hot coffee**, please.
8. Alright, just a moment, please.
9. Thank you!

✤ In Thailand, drinking a glass of Nam Dok Anchan, a vibrant blue tea made from butterfly pea flowers, is believed to bring clarity and calmness to the mind.

Important Reminder Before Starting Lesson 7

* * *

Congratulations on your progress so far! You are about to embark on a crucial stage of your learning: Phase No. 2.

Please follow these instructions starting from lesson 7:

- For each lesson from No. 7 onward, first translate the text of that lesson (No. 7, No. 8, etc.) from the target language into English.
- Then, go back 6 lessons and translate the English version of that lesson's text from English back into the target language, without referring to the original text.
- Compare your translation with the original text of that lesson and adjust if necessary.
- Read the original text of that lesson out loud, while listening to the audio.

This new phase is designed to activate the vocabulary you have already assimilated. Keep up the momentum and enjoy this enriching new phase of your learning!

วันที่ 7: คำคุณศัพท์บรรยาย I

1. สวัสดีครับ, คุณชอบดื่มอะไร?
2. ฉันชอบดื่มน้ำเย็น ๆ ครับ, และคุณล่ะ?
3. ฉันชอบกาแฟร้อน ๆ ค่ะ. คุณมาจากไหนคะ?
4. ฉันมาจากเมืองใหญ่ครับ, และคุณล่ะ?
5. ฉันอยู่ที่เมืองเล็ก ๆ ค่ะ. คุณทำอะไรคะ?
6. ฉันเป็นครูครับ. คุณชอบอะไร?
7. ฉันชอบดนตรีและกีฬาค่ะ. ยินดีที่ได้พบคุณ.
8. ยินดีที่ได้พบคุณเช่นกันครับ, ขอให้มีวันที่ดีนะคะ.

✤ In Thai, adjectives can also function as adverbs without any change in form when describing how an action is done.

1. sawatdī khrap, khun chọp dūem arai?

2. chan chọp dūem nām yen yen khrap, læ khun læ?

3. chan chọp kāfæ rọn rọn khā. khun mā cāk nai khā?

4. chan mā cāk meūang yai khrap, læ khun læ?

5. chan yû thī meūang lek lek khā. khun tham arai khā?

6. chan pen khrū khrap. khun chọp arai?

7. chan chọp dontrī læ kīlā khā. yin dī thī dāi phop khun.

8. yin dī thī dāi phop khun chēn kan khrap, khọ hai mī wan thī dī nā khā.

DAY 7: DESCRIPTIVE ADJECTIVES I 🌱

1. Hello, what do you like to drink?
2. I like to drink cold water, and you?
3. I like hot coffee. Where are you from?
4. I'm from a big city, and you?
5. I live in a small town. What do you do?
6. I'm a teacher. What do you like?
7. I like music and sports. Nice to meet you.
8. Nice to meet you too, have a good day.

♣ Thai literature often uses the adjective "luminous" to describe the mythical Naga serpent's scales, reflecting the creature's divine nature.

วันที่ 8: สถานที่และทิศทาง ตอนที่ 1 ✐

1. ที่นี่ร้อนไหม?
2. ไม่, ที่นี่เย็น.
3. ที่นั่นใกล้ไหม?
4. ไม่, ที่นั่นไกล.
5. ฉันต้องการไปที่นั่น.
6. ไปซ้ายหรือขวา?
7. ตรงไปแล้วไปซ้าย.
8. ทางนี้หรือทางนั้น?
9. ทางนี้ใกล้กว่า.

✤ In Thai, the word "ใน" (nai) means "in" and is used before a place to indicate location, like "ในบ้าน" (nai baan) means "in the house".

1. thỉ nỉ rón mǎi?
2. mâi, thỉ nỉ yen.
3. thỉ nán klâi mǎi?
4. mâi, thỉ nán klai.
5. chǎn tōngkān pai thỉ nán.
6. pai sái rǔe khwā?
7. trong pai lǽo pai sái.
8. thǎng nỉ rǔe thǎng nán?
9. thǎng nỉ klâi kwâ.

1. Is it hot **here**?
2. No, it's cool **here**.
3. Is **there** close?
4. No, **there** is far.
5. I want to go **there**.
6. Should I go **left** or **right**?
7. Go **straight** then turn **left**.
8. This way or **that way**?
9. **This way** is closer.

✤ In Thailand, the ancient city of Ayutthaya, once a flourishing Siamese trade and political capital, was so revered that it was known as the "Venice of the East" before its destruction in the 18th century.

วันที่ ๙: สถานที่และทิศทาง ๒

1. **หยุดที่นี่** คุณอยากดื่มอะไร?
2. ฉันอยากดื่มน้ำ และคุณล่ะ?
3. ฉันอยากได้กาแฟ **ข้างๆ** น้ำโซดา.
4. ร้านอยู่บนหรือ**ใต้**?
5. ร้านอยู่เหนือสวนสาธารณะ.
6. เราควรเลี้ยวซ้ายหรือเลี้ยวขวาที่สี่แยก?
7. **เลี้ยวขวาแล้วไปตรงไป.**
8. ร้านอยู่ทางซ้ายหรือทางขวา?
9. อยู่ข้างหลังธนาคาร.

✤ In Thai, to combine directions or locations, use the conjunction "และ" (láe) for "and" or "กับ" (gàp) for "with".

1. yut thī nī khun yāk dūem a-rai?
2. chan yāk dūem nām lae khun la?
3. chan yāk dāi kāfae khāng khái nām sōdā.
4. rān yū bon rēu tai?
5. rān yū neūa sān sāthāranikā.
6. rao khwān liō sāi rēu liō khwā thī sì yāk?
7. liō khwā lae pai trong pai.
8. rān yū thāng sāi rēu thāng khwā?
9. yū khāng lāng thānākhān.

1. **Stop here.** What would you like to drink?
2. I'd like some water. And you?
3. I'd like a coffee **next to** a soda.
4. Is the shop **above** or **below**?
5. The shop is **above** the public park.
6. Should we **turn left** or **turn right** at the intersection?
7. **Turn right** and then go **straight**.
8. Is the shop on the **left side** or the **right side**?
9. It's **behind** the bank.

✤ In Bangkok, the Grand Palace was once mistakenly painted pink overnight due to a mix-up in paint colors for a royal event.

วันที่ 10: คำถาม ✒

1. **ไหน** หนังสือของฉัน?
2. อยู่ข้างๆ คอมพิวเตอร์.
3. **ทำไม** มันอยู่ที่นั่น?
4. เพราะว่าฉันใช้มันเมื่อ ทำงานเสร็จ.
5. **อะไร** เป็นหนังสือที่คุณอ่าน?
6. หนังสือเกี่ยวกับการเรียนภาษา.
7. **ราคาเท่าไหร่?**
8. ไม่แพงมาก, แค่สองร้อยบาท.
9. **เย็น** นี้คุณว่างไหม, อยากไปซื้อหนังสือด้วยกันไหม?

✣ In Thai, to turn a statement into a question, often you just add "ไหม" (mai) at the end of the sentence.

1. **năi** năngsư̆ k̄hxng chạn?
2. xỳ **k̄hâng k̄hâng** khxmphiwteexr.
3. **thảmị̀** man xỳ thī̀ nạ̀n?
4. phr̄āwả chạn chî man **mềụ̄a** thảngān s̄r̆cch.
5. **àrị̀** pen năngsư̆ thī̀ khuṇ x̀ān?
6. năngsư̆ kī̀yw kạb kār rian phās̄̀ā.
7. **rākhā thêā h̄ịr̀?**
8. mị̀ phæng māk, khæ̀ s̄xng rôi bāth.
9. **yen** nī̂ khun wàng mị̀, x̀āk pai s̄ụ̂x năngsư̆ d̂wy kạn mị̀?

---

1. **Where** is my book?
2. It's **next to** the computer.
3. **Why** is it there?
4. Because I was using it **after** finishing my work.
5. **What** book are you reading?
6. A book about learning languages.
7. **How much** does it cost?
8. Not very expensive, just two hundred baht.
9. **Are you free** this evening, would you like to go buy a book together?

✤ In Thai culture, directly questioning someone's age or salary is often considered impolite, reflecting the nuanced art of asking questions respectfully.

CHALLENGE NO. 1

CHOOSE A THEME AND CREATE A COLLAGE OF PHOTOS OR IMAGES, NOTING THE CORRESPONDING WORD IN THAI.

อย่างมีความพยายาม ไม่มีอะไรที่ทำไม่ได้

With effort, nothing is impossible.

วันที่ 11: วันและเวลา

1. **วันนี้** เป็นวันอะไร?
2. **วันนี้** วันจันทร์ครับ.
3. **เวลา** ตอนนี้ กี่โมงแล้ว?
4. **ตอนนี้** เกือบสามโมงครึ่งครับ.
5. **พรุ่งนี้** คุณมีแผนอะไรไหม?
6. **พรุ่งนี้** ผมต้องไปทำงานครับ.
7. **เมื่อวาน** คุณทำอะไร?
8. **เมื่อวาน** ผมอยู่บ้านครับ.
9. แล้ว **มะรืนนี้** ล่ะ?
10. **มะรืนนี้** ผมว่างครับ.

✤ In Thai, to say the time, you put the word for hour (ชั่วโมง) after the number, like "3 ชั่วโมง" for 3 o'clock.

1. **Wan nî** pen wan à-rai?
2. **Wan nî** wan canthr khráp.
3. **Welā** ton nî kǐ mong lǽo?
4. **Ton nî** kèuap sām mong khrǔng khráp.
5. **Phrung nî** khun mī phæn à-rai mǎi?
6. **Phrung nî** phǒm tông pai tham ngān khráp.
7. **Mêua wan** khun tham à-rai?
8. **Mêua wan** phǒm yù bâan khráp.
9. Lǽo **ma-ruen nî** lǽ?
10. **Ma-ruen nî** phǒm wâng khráp.

1. **What day is it today?**
2. **Today** is Monday.
3. **What time** is it now?
4. **It's** almost half past three.
5. **Do you have any plans for tomorrow?**
6. **Tomorrow** I have to go to work.
7. **What did you do yesterday?**
8. **Yesterday** I stayed at home.
9. And **the day after tomorrow?**
10. **The day after tomorrow** I'm free.

✤ In Thailand, punctuality is often viewed with flexibility, embodying the cultural concept of "Thai time," where events and meetings start when everyone arrives.

วันที่ 12: วันในสัปดาห์ ✒

1. วันนี้วันอะไร?
2. วันนี้วันพุธครับ.
3. พรุ่งนี้ วันพฤหัสบดี ใช่ไหม?
4. ใช่ครับ, พรุ่งนี้วันพฤหัสบดี.
5. เมื่อวาน วันอังคาร ใช่ไหม?
6. ใช่ค่ะ, เมื่อวานวันอังคาร.
7. สุดสัปดาห์ วันเสาร์ และ วันอาทิตย์ ใช่ไหม?
8. ใช่ครับ, สุดสัปดาห์ คือ วันเสาร์ และ วันอาทิตย์.
9. ตกลงค่ะ, ขอบคุณครับ.

✤ In Thai, the subject often comes before the day of the week when talking about activities or events.

1. wan nî wan à-rai?
2. wan nî wan phut khráp.
3. phrûng nî wan phrēhạs̄bdī chì mı?
4. chì khráp, phrûng nî wan phrēhạs̄bdī.
5. mêuwan wan ạngkhān chì mı?
6. chì khà, mêuwan wan ạngkhān.
7. sùt s̄ạpdāh̄ wan s̄ār̄ læ wan ʿāthity̆ chì mı?
8. chì khráp, sùt s̄ạpdāh̄ khūx wan s̄ār̄ læ wan ʿāthity̆.
9. toklong khà, k̄hxbkhuṇ khráp.

1. **What day is it today?**
2. **Today is Wednesday.**
3. **Tomorrow is Thursday**, right?
4. Yes, **tomorrow is Thursday.**
5. **Yesterday was Tuesday**, right?
6. Yes, **yesterday was Tuesday.**
7. **The weekend is Saturday and Sunday**, right?
8. Yes, **the weekend** is **Saturday and Sunday.**
9. Okay, thank you.

♣ In Thailand, the names of the days are derived from the colors associated with different gods of the Hindu pantheon.

วันที่ 13: ครอบครัว I

1. **ครอบครัว** ของฉันมีใครบ้าง?
2. มี **แม่, พ่อ, พี่ชาย** และ **น้องสาว** ครับ/ค่ะ.
3. **พ่อแม่** สบายดีไหม?
4. สบายดีครับ/ค่ะ, **ขอบคุณ**!
5. **ย่า กับ ตา** ล่ะ?
6. พวกเขาก็สบายดีครับ/ค่ะ.
7. คุณมี **สามี** หรือ **ภรรยา** ไหม?
8. ยังไม่มีครับ/ค่ะ, ฉันยังโสด.
9. ฉันเข้าใจแล้ว, ขอบคุณที่บอกนะ.

✤ In Thai, to indicate a direct object, you often place it after the verb, for example, "I love mom" becomes "I love mom" (ฉันรักแม่).

1. **khrxbkhrūa** khxng chạn mī khır bāng?
2. mī **mæ̀, pʰx, pʰìchāy** læa **n̂xngsāw** khrạb/kʰà.
3. **pʰxmæ̀** s̄bāydī h̄ịm?
4. s̄bāydī khrạb/kʰà, **k̄hxbkhuṇ**!
5. **yā kạb tā** l̀ạ?
6. phwk kheā k̄h s̄bāydī khrạb/kʰà.
7. khun mī **s̄āmī** h̄rụ̄x **phrrnyā** h̄ịm?
8. yāng mị̀ mī khrạb/kʰà, chạn yāng s̄od.
9. chạn kheācı læw, k̄hxbkhuṇ thī̀ bxk ṇa.

1. Who is in **my family**?
2. There's **mom, dad, older brother**, and **younger sister**.
3. Are **your parents** doing well?
4. Yes, they are, **thank you**!
5. What about **grandma** and **grandpa**?
6. They are also doing well.
7. Do you have a **husband** or **wife**?
8. Not yet, I'm still single.
9. I see, thank you for letting me know.

✤ In traditional Thai families, it's common for multiple generations to live under one roof, fostering a strong sense of community and familial support.

วันที่ 14: ครอบครัว II ✐

1. สวัสดีครับ **ลูกพี่ลูกน้อง** คุณชื่ออะไรครับ?
2. สวัสดีค่ะ ฉันชื่อนกค่ะ และคุณล่ะ?
3. ฉันชื่อบอยครับ คุณเป็น **หลานสาว** ของใครครับ?
4. ฉันเป็น **หลานสาว** ของ **ป้า** ค่ะ
5. อ้อ ฉันเป็น **หลานชาย** ของ **ลุง** ครับ
6. น่าสนใจจังค่ะ คุณทำอะไรอยู่ตอนนี้คะ?
7. ตอนนี้ฉันเป็น **เพื่อนร่วมงาน** กับ **หุ้นส่วน** ครอบครัวครับ
8. ว้าว ดูเหมือนเราจะมีอะไรคล้ายกันนะคะ ยินดีที่ได้พบ
   คุณนะคะ
9. ยินดีที่ได้พบคุณเช่นกันครับ ขอให้มีวันที่ดีนะคะ

✤ In Thai, to indicate an indirect object, like telling whom you give something to, you often use the word "ให้" (hâi) before the person.

1. sawatdī khrap **lūk phī lūk n̂xng** khun chụ̄ xarị khrap?
2. sawatdī khà chạn chụ̄ nōk khà læa khun lạ?
3. chạn chụ̄ bxy khrap khun pen **h̄lān̄s̄āw** k̄hxng khray khrap?
4. chạn pen **h̄lān̄s̄āw** k̄hxng **pā** khà
5. x̀x chạn pen **h̄lānchāy** k̄hxng **lung** khrap
6. nà s̄nj chạng khà khun thả xarị xy thī̀ nī̂ khá?
7. thī̀ nī̂ chạn pen **ph̄ụ̀xn rwmngān** kạb **h̄ûns̄̀wn** khrxbkhrạw khrap
8. wāw dū h̄emụ̄̀n rao cā mī xarị khl̂āy kạn ná khà yindī thī̀ dị̂ phb khun ná khà
9. yindī thī̀ dị̂ phb khun chên kạn khrap k̄hx h̄ı̂ mī wạn thī̀ dī ná khà

DAY 14: FAMILY II

1. Hello **cousin**, what's you___ __e?
2. Hello, my name is Nok. A__ __ou?
3. My name is Boy. Whose **niece** are you?
4. I am the **niece** of my **aunt**.
5. Oh, I am the **nephew** of my **uncle**.
6. That's interesting. What are you doing right now?
7. Right now, I am **working with a business partner** in the family business.
8. Wow, it seems we have something in common. Nice to meet you.
9. Nice to meet you too. Have a great day.

✤ In Thailand, the Songkran Festival, also known as the Thai New Year, is a time when families gather to throw water on each other, symbolizing the washing away of bad luck and misfortunes.

วันที่ 15: ตัวเลข 1 ถึง 10

1. สวัสดีครับ วันนี้วันอะไรครับ?
2. วันนี้วันจันทร์ค่ะ
3. คุณมีแผนอะไรบ้างครับ?
4. ฉันจะไปเจอเพื่อนร่วมงานค่ะ
5. เข้าใจแล้วครับ คุณจะไปกี่โมงครับ?
6. ฉันจะไปสองโมงค่ะ
7. ดีมากครับ ฉันมีหุ้นส่วนสามคน
8. ว้าว นั่นเยอะมากเลยครับ
9. ใช่ค่ะ แต่เราทำงานดีมากค่ะ

✤ In Thai, to say how many items you have, place the number after the noun and use the verb "มี" (mee) for "to have" in the present tense.

1. Sawasdī khrap Wan nî wan àrai khrap?
2. Wan nî wan canthǹ khà
3. Khun mī phæn àrai bâng khrap?
4. Chǎn cà paí cēn pheǔan rūam ngān khà
5. Khâo chai lǽo khrap Khun cà paí kī mōng khrap?
6. Chǎn cà paí sōng mōng khà
7. Dī māk khrap Chǎn mī hûn sǎm khon
8. Wâo Nan yòe māk lēi khrap
9. Châi khà Tæ rao tham ngān dī māk khà

1. Hello, what day is it today?
2. Today is Monday.
3. Do you have any plans?
4. I'm going to meet a coworker.
5. I see. What time will you go?
6. I will go at two o'clock.
7. That's great. I have three partners.
8. Wow, that's a lot.
9. Yes, but we work very well together.

✤ In Thailand, the number 9 is considered incredibly lucky because it sounds like the word for "progress" in Thai.

วันที่ 16: ตัวเลข 11 ถึง 20 🌾

1. วันนี้ครอบครัวเรามีกี่คน?
2. **สิบเอ็ด** คนครับ, รวม **ย่า** กับ **ตา** ด้วย
3. แล้วเราจะดื่มอะไรดี?
4. **พ่อ ชอบดื่ม เบียร์, แม่ ชอบ น้ำ**
5. **พี่ชาย** กับ **น้องชาย**?
6. พวกเขาชอบ **โซดา** ครับ
7. แล้ว **พี่สาว** ล่ะ?
8. เธอชอบ **ชา** ค่ะ
9. ดีครับ, เรามีเครื่องดื่มพอสำหรับทุกคนแล้ว

❖ In Thai, to form numbers from 11 to 19, start with "sip" (10) and then add the number 1 to 9 after it, like "sip et" for 11.

1. Wannî khrxbkhrūa rao mī kī khn?
2. **Ŝibxd** khn khrạb, rūam **ŷā** kạb **tā** d̂wy
3. Læ̂w rao c̀ā deụ̄m xarị dī?
4. **Ph̀x** chxb deụ̄m **bīa, mæ̀ chxb n̂ả**
5. **Phî chāy** kạb **n̂xngchāy**?
6. Phūak kheā chxb **sōdā** khrạb
7. Læ̂w **phîs̄āw** l̀ạ?
8. Theū chxb **chā** kh̀ā
9. Dī khrạb, rao mī kherụ̀xngdeụ̄m phxs̄ảbhrụb thukkhn læw

1. How many people are in our family today?
2. **Eleven** people, including **grandma** and **grandpa**.
3. What should we drink?
4. **Dad** likes **beer**, **Mom likes water**.
5. What about **older brother** and **younger brother**?
6. They like **soda**.
7. And **older sister**?
8. She likes **tea**.
9. Great, we have enough drinks for everyone.

✤ In Thailand, children play a game called "Sab Suriya," where they sing a rhyme and hop through patterns drawn on the ground, counting each leap to reach the sun.

วันที่ 17: ช้อปปิ้ง I

1. วันนี้เราจะไปตลาดกันไหม?
2. อยากไปร้านค้าไหนล่ะ?
3. ฉันอยากซื้อเสื้อใหม่.
4. เรามาดูที่นี่สิ. ราคาไม่แพงมาก.
5. แต่มันยังไม่ถูกเท่าที่ฉันต้องการ.
6. ดูสิ, ที่นี่มีการลดราคา.
7. มีส่วนลดเพิ่มเติมถ้าจ่ายด้วยเงินสดหรือไม่?
8. ใช่, แต่ถ้าจ่ายด้วยบัตรเครดิตจะไม่ได้ส่วนลดเพิ่ม.
9. โอเค, ฉันจะจ่ายด้วยเงินสด.

✤ In Thai, to make a sentence negative, add "ไม่" (mai) before the verb, like "I don't want" becomes "ฉันไม่ต้องการ" (chan mai tong-gaan).

1. Wan nî ráo cà pāi **tàlàat** kan măi?
2. Yàak pāi **ráan khâ** năi là?
3. Chăn yàak **súê** sûea mài.
4. Ráo mā **dū** thî nî sì. Rákhā mâi **phaeng** mâak.
5. Dtàe man yang mâi **thùk** thâo thî chăn tôngkān.
6. Dū sì, thî nî mī kaan **lót rákhā**.
7. Mī **sàuan lót** phîm tûm thâa cài dûay **ngoen sŏt** rĕu mâi?
8. Châi, dtàe thâa cài dûay **bat kradìt** cà mâi dâi sàuan lót phîm.
9. O khē, chăn cà cài dûay ngoen sŏt.

1. Are we going to the **market** today?
2. Which **store** do you want to visit?
3. I want to **buy** a new shirt.
4. Let's **look** here. The prices aren't very **expensive**.
5. But it's still not as **cheap** as I would like.
6. Look, there's a **sale** here.
7. Is there an additional **discount** if I pay with **cash**?
8. Yes, but if you pay with a **credit card**, you won't get the extra discount.
9. Okay, I'll pay with cash.

✤ In Thai traditional markets, it's common to greet vendors with a smile before negotiating, as friendliness can lead to better prices.

วันที่ 18: ช้อปปิ้ง ครั้งที่สอง

1. ฉันอยากซื้อเสื้อผ้าและเครื่องประดับที่นี่.
2. ดีค่ะ, **รถเข็นหรือตะกร้า**คะ?
3. ตะกร้าค่ะ, ขอบคุณ.
4. คุณลองดูที่ห้องลองเสื้อผ้าได้นะคะ.
5. **เสื้อแจ็คเก็ต**นี้ราคาเท่าไหร่คะ?
6. สี่พันบาทค่ะ. และแว่นตากันแดดนี้ล่ะ?
7. สองพันบาทค่ะ.
8. โอเคค่ะ, ฉันจะเอาทั้งสอง. ชำระที่**เคาน์เตอร์**ได้ไหม?
9. ได้ค่ะ, ตามฉันมาค่ะ.

✤ In Thai, to form a question about shopping, you often add "ไหม (mai)" at the end of the sentence.

1. Chạn xỳāk sụ̂x **šeụ̂x phā** læa **khreụ̂xng pradạb** thỉ nỉ.
2. Dī khā, **rth khen** rū **tạkrā** khá?
3. **Tạkrā** khả, k̀hxbkhuṇ.
4. Khun lọng dū thỉ **ĥxng lọng šeụ̂x phā** dỉ ná khà.
5. **Šeụ̂x jæk kèt** nỉ **rākhā** thảhỉr̀ khá?
6. Sì pạn bāth khà. Læa **wæ̀n tā kạn dæd** nỉ lè?
7. Šxng pạn bāth khà.
8. Okh khà, chạn cā thạng sxng. Chạmrạ thỉ **khāntêr** dỉ mỉ?
9. Dỉ khà, tām chạn mā khà.

78

1. I want to buy **clothes** and **accessories** here.
2. Sure, **a cart** or **a basket**?
3. **A basket**, please, thank you.
4. You can try them on in the **fitting room**.
5. How much is this **jacket**?
6. Four thousand baht. And these **sunglasses**?
7. Two thousand baht.
8. Okay, I'll take both. Can I pay at the **counter**?
9. Yes, follow me, please.

✤ In Thailand, the world's first floating market, Damnoen Saduak, combines shopping with cultural immersion, dating back to the late 19th century.

วันที่ 19: การขนส่ง 1

1. ฉันจะไปสนามบิน ฉันควรใช้แท็กซี่หรือรถบัสดี?
2. แท็กซี่จะสะดวกกว่า แต่ถ้าอยากประหยัด ใช้รถบัสก็ได้
3. ถ้าฉันอยากไปสถานีรถไฟล่ะ?
4. จากสนามบินนั้น ใช้รถไฟสะดวกที่สุด
5. แล้วถ้าจะไปเที่ยวทะเลล่ะ? ฉันควรใช้เรือหรือรถยนต์?
6. ถ้าไปกับเพื่อนหลายคน ใช้รถยนต์ดีกว่า แต่ถ้าอยาก
   สัมผัสบรรยากาศทะเลจริงๆ ใช้เรือน่าจะดี
7. ฉันอยากลองขี่จักรยานในเมืองดูบ้าง
8. นั่นก็เป็นความคิดที่ดี สามารถเช่าจักรยานได้ที่หลายๆ ที่
   ในเมือง

✤ In Thai, to say "I go by car," you use the structure "I go car," adding the word for "by" before the mode of transport.

1. chạn cà pī **sānām bin** chạn khwān chai **thǽksǐ** rū **rōt bàt** dī?
2. **thǽksǐ** cà sādwàk kwǎ thâ chā yàk pràyòt chai **rōt bàt** kô dai
3. thâ chạn yàk pai **sāthānī rōt fai** là?
4. càk **sānām bin** nán chai **rōt fai** sādwàk thīsùt
5. láew thâ cà pai thiâw thālè là? chạn khwān chai **rūa** rū **rōt yon**?
6. thâ pai kap phûan lāi khon chai **rōt yon** dī kwǎ thâ yàk sǎmphât ban yā kā
   thālè cing cing chai **rūa** nâ chà dī
7. chạn yàk lōng kī **čhakrayān** nai mūang dū bâng
8. nân kô pēn khām khit thī dī sāmāt châo **čhakrayān** dai thī lāi lāi thī nai
   mūang

1. I'm going to the **airport**. Should I use a **taxi** or a **bus**?
2. A **taxi** would be more convenient, but if you want to save money, a **bus** is also an option.
3. What if I want to go to the **train station**?
4. From the **airport**, taking a **train** is the most convenient.
5. And what about going to the beach? Should I use a **boat** or a **car**?
6. If you're going with a group of friends, a **car** would be better. But if you want to truly experience the sea atmosphere, a **boat** might be a good choice.
7. I'd like to try riding a **bicycle** around the city.
8. That's a great idea. You can rent **bicycles** at many places in the city.

✤ In Thailand, tuk-tuks, originally named after the sound of their engine, offer a vibrant and nimble way to navigate through bustling city streets.

วันที่ 20: การขนส่ง 2

1. ออกเดินทาง เมื่อไหร่?
2. ถึง สนามบิน เมื่อไหร่?
3. บัตรโดยสาร แพง ไหม?
4. ไม่, บัตรโดยสาร ถูก.
5. ตั๋ว อยู่ที่ อาคารผู้โดยสาร ประตู ไหน?
6. ประตู 3.
7. สัมภาระ และ กระเป๋าเดินทาง อยู่ที่ไหน?
8. อยู่ที่ ประตู 4.
9. กระเป๋าเป้ ล่าช้า ไหม?
10. ไม่, ไม่ ล่าช้า.

✤ To ask where someone is going in Thai, start with "ไป" (go) followed by the place and end with "ไหม" (question marker), like "ไปโรงเรียนไหม?" (Are you going to school?).

1. xxk dein thāng meůa rài?
2. theūng sānām bin meůa rài?
3. bat doī sān phæng mǎi?
4. mǎi, bat doī sān thūk.
5. tǔa yǔ thī ākhān phǔ doī sān pratu nǎi?
6. pratu 3.
7. samphāra læ krāpǎo dein thāng yǔ thīnǎi?
8. yǔ thī pratu 4.
9. krāpǎo phé lāchā mǎi?
10. mǎi, mǎi lāchā.

1. **Departing** when?
2. Arrive at the **airport** when?
3. Is the **ticket** expensive?
4. No, the **ticket** is cheap.
5. Where is the **ticket** at the **passenger terminal**? Which gate?
6. Gate 3.
7. Where are the **luggage** and **suitcases**?
8. At **gate** 4.
9. Is the **backpack** delayed?
10. No, it's not **delayed**.

✤ In Thailand, the first public bus service was introduced in Bangkok in 1931, initially operated with a fleet of just 30 buses.

CHALLENGE NO. 2

WRITE A SHORT TEXT IN THAI
INTRODUCING YOURSELF AND
EXPLAINING WHY YOU ARE LEARNING
THIS LANGUAGE.

การเรียนรู้ไม่มีวันสิ้นสุด

Learning never ends.

วันที่ 21: สถานที่และที่ตั้ง I 🌱

1. วันนี้เราจะไป**โรงเรียน**กันไหม?
2. ไม่, วันนี้ฉันต้องไป**ธนาคาร**และ**ร้านขายยา**ก่อน.
3. แล้วพรุ่งนี้ล่ะ? เราไปสวนสาธารณะได้ไหม?
4. ได้สิ, พรุ่งนี้เราไปสวนสาธารณะกัน.
5. ตอนนี้ฉันอยู่ที่บ้าน. คุณอยู่ที่ไหน?
6. ฉันอยู่ที่สำนักงาน. แต่เดี๋ยวฉันจะไปร้านอาหารก่อนกลับ.
7. ดีจัง, ฉันก็หิวแล้ว. เจอกันที่ร้านอาหารนะ.
8. โอเค, เจอกัน!

✤ To tell someone to go to a place in Thai, start the sentence with "ไป" (go) followed by the location.

1. Wanní̂ rao cà pāi **rōngrīan** kan h̄ịm?
2. Mị̀, wanní̂ c̄hạn t̂xng pāi **thānākhān** læa **r̂ān khāy yā** k̀xn.
3. Læa phrûngní̂ la? Rao pāi **s̄wn s̄āthārṇā** dị̂ h̄ịm?
4. Dị̂ s̄ị̀, phrûngní̂ rao pāi **s̄wn s̄āthārṇā** kan.
5. Tawní̂ c̄hạn yù thī **b̂ān**. Khun yù thīh̄ịn?
6. C̄hạn yù thī **s̄ảnạkngān**. Tæ̀ dǐyw c̄hạn cà pāi **r̂ān 'āh̄ār** k̀xn klạb.
7. Dī cạng, c̄hạn k̆ h̄iw læw. Cex kan thī **r̂ān 'āh̄ār** ná.
8. Ok, cex kan!

1. Are we going to **school** today?
2. No, today I have to go to the **bank** and the **pharmacy** first.
3. What about tomorrow? Can we go to the **park**?
4. Sure, we'll go to the **park** tomorrow.
5. I'm at **home** right now. Where are you?
6. I'm at the **office**. But I'll go to a **restaurant** before heading back.
7. Great, I'm hungry too. See you at the **restaurant** then.
8. Okay, see you!

✤ Thailand's Ayutthaya Historical Park, once a Siamese capital, is now a UNESCO World Heritage Site, showcasing the grandeur of ancient Siam.

วันที่ 22: คุณศัพท์ 2

1. วันนี้วันอะไรคะ?
2. วันจันทร์ครับ
3. โรงเรียนของเรา**ใหญ่**หรือ**เล็ก**คะ?
4. **ใหญ่**ครับ
5. รถบัสมา**เร็ว**หรือ**ช้า**คะ?
6. มา**ช้า**ครับ
7. สนามบิน**กว้าง**หรือ**ยาว**ครับ?
8. **กว้าง**ครับ
9. ขอบคุณครับ
10. ยินดีครับ

✤ In Thai, to form an exclamatory sentence with an adjective, place the adjective before the noun and add "แหละ" (làe) at the end for emphasis, like "สวยแหละ!" (Beautiful indeed!).

1. Wan nî wan à-rai khá?
2. Wan canthr̀ khráp
3. Rongrīan khǒng rao **yài** rǔe **lék** khá?
4. **Yài** khráp
5. Roth bát mā **reo** rǔe **chá** khá?
6. Mā **chá** khráp
7. Šnām bin **kwāng** rǔe **yāo** khráp?
8. **Kwāng** khráp
9. Khxbkhuṇ khráp
10. Yindī khráp

1. What day is it today?
2. It's Monday.
3. Is our school **big** or **small**?
4. It's **big**.
5. Does the bus come **quickly** or **slowly**?
6. It comes **slowly**.
7. Is the airport **wide** or **long**?
8. It's **wide**.
9. Thank you.
10. You're welcome.

✤ In Thailand, the stunning Phraya Nakhon Cave features a hidden pavilion bathed in sunlight through its open ceiling, creating a mystical atmosphere.

วันที่ 23: คุณศัพท์ ชุดที่ 3 ✎

1. วันนี้อากาศ**เย็น**มาก
2. ใช่, แต่ฉันชอบเพราะมันทำให้รู้สึก**สงบ**
3. คุณเตรียม**เสื้อแข็ง**ไปด้วยไหม?
4. ใช่, และฉันยังเอา**ผ้าห่มนุ่ม**ด้วย
5. ดีมาก, อย่าลืม**บัตรโดยสาร**นะ
6. แน่นอน, ฉันเตรียม**เต็ม**แล้ว
7. เราจะ**ออกเดินทาง**เมื่อไหร่?
8. **ถึงอาคารผู้โดยสาร**ตอนเช้า
9. โอเค, ฉันหวังว่าจะไม่**หนัก**เกินไปในการพกพา

✤ In Thai, to make an adjective negative, place "ไม่" (mai) before the adjective.

1. wan nî 'ākāt **yen** māk
2. chai, dæ̀t chăn chɔ̂p phrɔ̌ mǎn tham hai rû̂ sūk **sŏng bɔ̌**
3. khun trīam **sūa khǎeng** pai dūai mǎi?
4. chai, læa chǎn yang 'ao **phâ hǎm nûm** dūai
5. dī māk, yà lǎm **bat dōi sān** na
6. æ̀ nɛ̂nɔ̌n, chǎn trīam **tem** læo
7. rao cā **'ɔ̀k dointhāng** mǔa hai?
8. **thǔeng** 'ākān phū dōi sān tɔ̂n cháo
9. ōkhe, chǎn hwǎng wā cǎ mâi **nak** kōen pai nai kān phōk phā

DAY 23: ADJECTIVES III

1. Today, the weather is **cold**.
2. Yes, but I like it because it feels **peaceful**.
3. Did you bring a **jacket** with you?
4. Yes, and I also brought a **soft blanket**.
5. Great, don't forget your **ticket**.
6. Of course, I've prepared **everything**.
7. When do we **depart**?
8. **Arrive** at the passenger building in the morning.
9. Okay, I hope it won't be too **heavy** to carry.

✦ Thai poetry often uses "floating adjectives," where descriptive words intriguingly precede or follow their subjects, creating a fluid and vivid imagery unique to the language's literary style.

วันที่ 24: สี

1. สวัสดีครับ วันนี้ฉันอยากซื้อเสื้อสีอะไรดีนะ?
2. ฉันว่าสี**เขียว**ดูสงบดีนะ หรือว่าจะเป็นสี**น้ำเงิน**?
3. อืม, แต่ฉันชอบสี**แดง**นะ เพราะมันดูแข็งแรง.
4. แต่สี**เหลือง**ก็ดูสดใสดีนะ มันทำให้รู้สึกเย็นๆ.
5. จริงๆ ฉันก็ชอบสี**ดำ** เพราะมันดูนุ่มนวล.
6. หรือว่าเราจะลองดูสี**ขาว**? มันดูสะอาดและเรียบง่าย.
7. ฉันคิดว่าสี**น้ำตาล**ก็ไม่เลวนะ มันดูอบอุ่น.
8. หรือสี**ชมพู**ก็ดูน่ารักดี แต่สี**เทา**ก็ดูเท่ห์.
9. สุดท้ายนี้ สี**ส้ม**ก็ดูสดใสและมีชีวิตชีวานะ.

✤ In Thai, colors are usually spelled with the word "สี" (sǐi) in front, like "สีแดง" (sǐi daeng) for "red".

1. sawatdī khrap wan nî chǎn yàk sû̂ sû̂a sǐi àrai dī na?
2. chǎn wâ sǐi **khǐaw** dū sngop dī na ȟrŭ̄x wâ cà bpen sǐi **námngoen**?
3. eūm, tæ̀ chǎn chôb sǐi **dæng** na phrô man dū khæng raeng.
4. tæ̀ sǐi **lǔang** k̂dū sadaj dī na man tham hâi rû̂ sùk yen yen.
5. cìng cìng chǎn k̂d chôb sǐi **dam** phrô man dū nùm nuan.
6. ȟrŭ̄x wâ rao cà long dū sǐi **khǎw**? man dū s̀ād læa rǐap ngǎi.
7. chǎn khid wâ sǐi **námtān** k̂ mâi leo na man dū `ob `un.
8. ȟrŭ̄x sǐi **chomphū** k̂dū nāṛak dī tæ̀ sǐi **thāo** k̂dū thê.
9. s̄udthāy nî sǐi **s̄om** k̂dū sadaj læa mī chīwit chīwa na.

1. Hello! What color shirt should I buy today?
2. I think **green** looks peaceful, or maybe **blue**?
3. Hmm, but I like **red** because it looks strong.
4. But **yellow** also looks bright and feels cool.
5. Actually, I also like **black** because it looks soft.
6. Or should we consider **white**? It looks clean and simple.
7. I think **brown** is not bad either; it looks warm.
8. Or **pink** looks cute, but **gray** looks cool.
9. Lastly, **orange** looks bright and lively too.

✤ In Thailand, each day of the week is associated with a specific color, believed to bring good luck; for example, yellow is for Monday, the day of the King's birth.

วันที่ 25: อิเล็กทรอนิกส์และเทคโนโลยี I ✐

1. สวัสดี
2. สวัสดีตอนบ่าย คุณใช้ **อินเทอร์เน็ต** บน **สมาร์ทโฟน** หรือ **คอมพิวเตอร์?**
3. ฉันใช้บน **แล็ปท็อป** และเชื่อมต่อ **ไวไฟ** เพื่อเข้า **โซเชียล เน็ตเวิร์ก.**
4. คุณมี **แอปพลิเคชัน** โปรดไหม?
5. มีครับ, ฉันชอบใช้ **เบราว์เซอร์** เพื่อดูข้อมูลและ **ดาวน์โหลด** ข้อมูล.
6. ฉันก็ชอบส่ง **อีเมล** ผ่านสมาร์ทโฟน.
7. ดีมากเลย
8. ใช่ครับ, สะดวกมากๆ
9. ลาก่อน

✤ In Thai, when writing about electronics and technology, we don't use commas between items in a list, but instead, we use the word "และ" (and) before the last item.

1. sawasdī
2. sawasdī tawn bàay, khun chái **inthēnet** bon **smāt thǫn** rēu **khomphūtēr?**
3. chan chái bon **laep thóp** læa chēum tô **wai fai** pheûa khao **sōchēial netwérk.**
4. khun mī **æpphlikhēch'an** prōd mǎi?
5. mī khrap, chan chǫp chái **brǫsēo** pheûa dū khana læa **dāwnlōd** khana.
6. chan kǭ chǫp sǫng **īmem** phān smāt thǫn.
7. dī māk loei
8. chai khrap, sàdwāk māk māk
9. lā kòn

1. Hello
2. Good afternoon, do you use **internet** on a **smartphone** or **computer**?
3. I use it on a **laptop** and connect to **Wi-Fi** to access **social networks**.
4. Do you have a favorite **application**?
5. Yes, I like using a **browser** to view information and **download** data.
6. I also like sending **emails** through my smartphone.
7. That's great.
8. Yes, it's very convenient.
9. Goodbye

♣ Thailand is the birthplace of Red Bull, the world-famous energy drink, originally created to help keep truck drivers awake.

วันที่ 26: เดือนและฤดูกาล ✑

1. ตอนนี้เดือนอะไรคะ?
2. **กุมภาพันธ์** ครับ.
3. อากาศเป็นยังไงบ้างคะ?
4. อากาศ**เย็น**ครับ.
5. คุณชอบ**กุมภาพันธ์**ไหมคะ?
6. ใช่ครับ, ผมชอบมากเพราะอากาศ**เย็น**.
7. คุณคิดว่ามีนา**คม**จะ**ร้อน**ไหมคะ?
8. **อาจจะ**ครับ, แต่ผมก็ชอบ.
9. ตกลงค่ะ, ขอบคุณครับ.

✤ In Thai, to indicate an action happened in the past, often the word "**แล้ว**" (láew) is added after the verb or at the end of the sentence.

1. tawn níi deūan a-rai kha?
2. **kumphāphan** khrap.
3. ākāt pen yang ngai bāng kha?
4. ākāt **yen** khrap.
5. khun chǝ̌ep **kumphāphan** mǎi kha?
6. chai khrap, phǒm chǝ̌ep māk phrǎ ākāt **yen**.
7. khun khit wā **mīnākhom** cā **rǒn** mǎi kha?
8. **āt cā** khrap, tǣ phǒm kǝ̂ chǝ̌ep.
9. tok long khâ, khǒpkhun khrap.

1. What month is it now?
2. **February**.
3. How's the weather?
4. The weather is **cool**.
5. Do you like **February**?
6. Yes, I really like it because the weather is **cool**.
7. Do you think **March** will be **hot**?
8. **Maybe**, but I still like it.
9. Okay, thank you.

✣ In Thailand, the Loi Krathong Festival involves floating baskets on water to honor the water spirits and let go of misfortunes.

วันที่ 27: ไม่มีเดือนและฤดูกาลอีกต่อไป 🌱

1. วันนี้อากาศเป็นอย่างไรบ้าง?
2. หนาวมาก! แต่ไม่มีฤดูใบไม้ร่วงหรือฤดูใบไม้ผลิอีกต่อไป แล้ว.
3. พยากรณ์บอกว่าจะมีฝนหรือแดด ในพฤศจิกายนนี้ไหม?
4. ไม่แน่นอนเลย ตอนนี้ทุกอย่างเปลี่ยนไปหมดแล้ว.
5. ฉันคิดถึงฤดูร้อนและฤดูใบไม้ผลิจัง.
6. ใช่, ฉันก็เหมือนกัน. ชอบเวลาที่อากาศอบอุ่น.
7. ตอนนี้เราต้องปรับตัวให้เข้ากับการไม่มีธันวาคมและ พฤศจิกายนแล้ว.
8. ใช่, ขอบคุณ! เราต้องเรียนรู้ที่จะอยู่กับมัน.

✤ To talk about future events in Thai, add "จะ" (jà) before the verb, like "I will go" becomes "ฉันจะไป" (chăn jà bpai).

1. wan nī **ākāt** pen yāng rai bāng?
2. **nāo** māk! tæ̀ mī **rūdu bai māi rộng** rū **rūdu bai māi phọn** īk tộ pai lǣo.
3. **phayākon** bòk wā cā mī **fọn** rū **dæd** nai **phrɯtsachikāyon** nī māi?
4. māi nǣnọn loei ton nī thuk yang plīan pai mot lǣo.
5. chan khid thūng **rūdu rộn** læ **rūdu bai māi phọn** chang.
6. chāi, chan kộ rūan kan. chộp welā thī **ākāt** òp ùn.
7. ton nī rao tộng prap tua hai khao kap kān māi mī **thanwākom** læ **phrɯtsachikāyon** lǣo.
8. chāi, khộpkhun! rao tộng rīan rū thī cā yù kap man.

98

1. How's the **weather** today?
2. **Cold** a lot! But there's no **autumn** or **spring** anymore.
3. Does the **forecast** say if there will be **rain** or **sun** in **November**?
4. Not sure at all, everything has changed now.
5. I miss **summer** and **spring** so much.
6. Yes, me too. I like it when the **weather** is warm.
7. Now we have to adjust to not having **December** and **November** anymore.
8. Yes, thank you! We have to learn to live with it.

♣ In Thailand, the Songkran Festival marks the Thai New Year in April, where people celebrate by engaging in massive, country-wide water fights.

วันที่ 28: ความรู้สึก I 🌿

1. สวัสดีครับ คุณรู้สึกอย่างไรบ้างวันนี้?
2. ผมรู้สึก**สุข**ใจมากครับ เพราะวันนี้ผมได้**ผ่อนคลาย**หลังจากทำงานเสร็จ
3. นั่นดีจังเลยค่ะ แต่ฉันกลับรู้สึก**เศร้า**และ**กังวล**เล็กน้อย
4. เหรอครับ? เกิดอะไรขึ้นหรือครับ?
5. ฉันรู้สึก**เหงา**เพราะอยู่คนเดียว แต่พอได้คุยกับคุณ ฉันก็เริ่มรู้สึก**ร่าเริง**ขึ้น
6. นั่นสิ การได้คุยกันทำให้เรา**ภูมิ**ใจและ**ตื่นเต้น**ที่ได้แบ่งปันความรู้สึก
7. ใช่ครับ และตอนนี้ผมไม่รู้สึก**โกรธ**หรือ**กระวนกระวาย**เลย
8. ดีใจด้วยค่ะ ขอให้เราทั้งคู่มีวันที่ดีและ**ผ่อนคลาย**ต่อไป
9. ขอบคุณครับ ยินดีที่ได้พบคุณ

✤ In Thai, the indicative mood is used to express factual statements or beliefs, such as "I am happy" or "She feels sad."

1. sawatdī khrap khun rûsuk yāng rai bāng wan nī?
2. phǒm rûsuk **sukhchai** māk khrap phrǎ chā wan nī phǒm dāi **phǒn klai** lǎng chāk tham ngān sèt
3. nan dī jang lœi khà thæ̀ chǎn klap rûsuk **sǎo** læ **kangwan** lek nǒi
4. hǒrē khrap? kìd àrài khǔn hrǔ̀ khrap?
5. chǎn rûsuk **ngǎo** phrā yǔ khon dīo thæ̀ phǒ dāi khui kap khun chǎn kǒ̌ štārt rûsuk **rāreng** khǔn
6. nan sī kǎn dāi khui kan tham hî khao rao **phūmīchai** læ **tǔn tên** thî dāi bèng phan khwām rûsuk
7. chî khrap læ thî nī phǒm māi rûsuk **krôth** hrǔ̀ **krāwan krāwāi** lœi
8. dī chai dūai khà khǒ̌ hî rao thang khû mī wan thî dī læ **phǒn klai** txng pai
9. khǒpkhun khrap yindī thî dāi phob khun

1. Hello! How are you feeling today?
2. I'm feeling **very happy** because today I got to **relax** after finishing work.
3. That's wonderful! But I feel a bit **sad** and **worried**.
4. Oh? What happened?
5. I feel **lonely** because I'm alone, but talking to you makes me start to feel **cheerful**.
6. Exactly, talking to each other makes us feel **proud** and **excited** to share our feelings.
7. Yes, and now I don't feel **angry** or **anxious** at all.
8. I'm glad to hear that. May we both have a good and **relaxing** day ahead.
9. Thank you. It's a pleasure to meet you.

✤ In Thailand, smiling is not just a sign of happiness but can also express a range of emotions including embarrassment, confusion, or apology.

วันที่ 29: ความรู้สึก II

1. **ฉันรู้สึกเครียด** มากเลย
2. ทำไมล่ะ? **ฉันกลัว** ว่าจะทำไม่ได้
3. **ฉันเข้าใจ** แต่อย่าวิตกกังวล นะ
4. แต่**ฉันสับสน** จริงๆ
5. ลอง**ผ่อนคลาย** ดูสิ
6. ถ้าสำเร็จ **ฉันจะดีใจ** มากๆ
7. แน่นอน **ฉันก็ปลื้ม** ด้วย
8. **ฉันรักคุณ** นะ
9. **ฉันคิดถึงคุณ** ด้วย

✤ In Thai, to express a command or request, use the verb at the beginning of the sentence without a subject.

1. **Chạn rûsuk khriiat** māk lēuy
2. Tham mai lạ? **Chạn klūa** wâ chà tham mâi dâi
3. **Chạn khâo cai** tæ̀ yà **witok kangwon** ná
4. Tæ̀ **chạn sǎp sǒn** cing cing
5. Lộng **ph̀xn klāi** dū sī
6. Thâ sǎmrec **chạn cà dī cai** māk māk
7. Ǎenxn **chạn k̲y plūm** dūay
8. **Chạn rạk khun** ná
9. **Chạn khit thụng khun** dūay

1. **I feel stressed** a lot
2. Why is that? **I'm afraid** that I won't be able to do it
3. **I understand** but don't **worry** too much
4. But **I'm really confused**
5. Try to **relax**
6. If I succeed, **I'll be very happy**
7. Of course, **I'll be pleased** too
8. **I love you**
9. **I miss you** too

✤ In Thailand, the epic poem "Phra Aphai Mani" by Sunthorn Phu, tells a captivating tale of love, adventure, and a magical flute that can charm both humans and mythical creatures alike.

วันที่ 30: ส่วนต่างๆ ของร่างกาย I

1. วันนี้ **หัว** ของฉันปวดมาก
2. ฉันเห็น **ผม** ของเธอยุ่งมาก
3. **ตา** ของฉันรู้สึกเครียด
4. **หู** ของฉันไม่ได้ยินเสียง
5. **จมูก** ของฉันไม่ได้กลิ่น
6. **ปาก** ของฉันแห้งมาก
7. **ฟัน** ของฉันเจ็บ
8. **มือ** และ **แขน** ของฉันอ่อนเพลีย
9. **ขา** ของฉันไม่อยากเดิน

✤ In Thai, when talking about body parts, use the subjunctive mood to express wishes or hypothetical situations, like "If I had stronger legs, I could run faster."

1. wan nī **hǔa** khǎng chan puat māk
2. chan hen **phǒm** khǎng thoe yung māk
3. **tā** khǎng chan rû seuk khriēt
4. **hū** khǎng chan mâi dâi yin sīang
5. **jamūk** khǎng chan mâi dâi klīn
6. **pāk** khǎng chan hǽng māk
7. **fan** khǎng chan jep
8. **mūe** læ **khæn** khǎng chan`xn phlīa
9. **khā** khǎng chan mâi yàk doēn

1. Today, **my head** hurts a lot.
2. I see **your hair** is very messy.
3. **My eyes** feel strained.
4. **My ears** can't hear sounds.
5. **My nose** can't smell.
6. **My mouth** is very dry.
7. **My teeth** hurt.
8. **My hands** and **arms** feel weak.
9. **My legs** don't want to walk.

✤ In Thailand, having a lighter skin tone is traditionally seen as a symbol of beauty and high social status, leading to the popularity of skin whitening products.

CHALLENGE NO. 3

CHOOSE A SHORT ARTICLE IN A THAI
NEWSPAPER AND TRANSLATE IT INTO
ENGLISH.

การสื่อสารเป็นสะพานของความเข้าใจ
Communication is the bridge of understanding.

วันที่ 31: ส่วนต่างๆ ของร่างกาย ภาค 2 🌱

1. วันนี้ **หลัง** ฉันเจ็บมาก
2. ทำไมล่ะ? ทำอะไรที่ **สำนักงาน** เหรอ?
3. ใช่, นั่งทำงานนานๆ แล้ว **หลัง** ก็เจ็บ
4. ลองไป **โรงพยาบาล** ดูไหม?
5. ฉันคิดว่าควรไป **ร้านขายยา** ก่อนดีกว่า
6. อาจจะต้องการยาบางอย่างสำหรับ **ผิวหนัง** หรือ **กล้ามเนื้อ**
7. ใช่, และฉันหวังว่ามันจะทำให้ฉัน **ผ่อนคลาย**
8. หวังว่าเธอจะรู้สึก **ดี** เร็วๆ นี้นะ
9. ขอบคุณมาก!

✤ If you touch your head, you say "หัว" in Thai.

1. wan nî **lang** chan cĕp māk
2. tham-mai ̀la? tham à-rai thī **sam-nák-ngān** ȟer?
3. chì, nâng tham-ngān nān-nān læw **lang** k̆ep
4. lǫng bpai **rōng-phá-yā-bān** du mị?
5. chan khid wâ chūa bpai **rán khāi yā** ̀kxn dī kwa
6. āc cà ̂thāng kān yā bāng xỳāng sam-rạb **phīw năng** ȓeu **klām ǹưe**
7. chì, læa chan hwāng wâ man cā tham ȟị chan **ph̀xn klāi**
8. hwāng wâ thè̆ cā rû̆ š̌k **dī** rew-rēw nî̌ ná
9. kȟxbkhuṇ māk!

1. Today, **my back** hurts a lot.
2. Why is that? Did you do something at the **office**?
3. Yes, sitting and working for long periods, and then **my back** starts hurting.
4. Have you considered going to the **hospital**?
5. I think it might be better to go to a **pharmacy** first.
6. You might need some medication for your **skin** or **muscles**.
7. Yes, and I hope it will help me **relax**.
8. I hope you feel **better** soon.
9. Thank you so much!

✤ In Thailand, the intricate finger movements in traditional dances are believed to convey the dance's story as much as the steps themselves.

วันที่ 32: เวลาและปฏิทิน 🍴

1. **วันนี้**เป็นวันอะไร?
2. **วันนี้**วันจันทร์ครับ.
3. เรามี**ปฏิทิน**ไหม?
4. มีครับ อยู่ที่นั่น.
5. คุณมี**ตารางเวลา**สำหรับ**สัปดาห์**นี้ไหม?
6. มีค่ะ ต้องการดู**เดือน**อะไร?
7. **เดือน**หน้าค่ะ.
8. ตกลงครับ แล้วเรามีนัดอะไรบ้างใน**เดือน**หน้า?
9. มีการประชุมสำคัญสองครั้งและเดินทางไปต่างจังหวัดหนึ่ง
   ครั้งค่ะ.

✤ In Thai, to express an action happening at a specific time, place the time expression at the beginning of the sentence, followed by the subject and verb in active voice.

1. **Wan** nî pen wan àrai?
2. **Wan** nî wan canthr khráp.
3. Rao mī **patithin** măi?
4. Mī khráp, yù thî nan.
5. Khun mī **tārang wēlā** sǎmphraph **sapdāh** nî mǎi?
6. Mī khà, tǒngkān du **duean** àrai?
7. **Duean** nà khà.
8. Toklong khráp, láeo rao mī nat àrai bāng nai **duean** nà?
9. Mī kān prachum sǎmkhan sǒng khrang láeo doēn thāng pai tàeng jangwat nùng khrang khà.

1. **What** day is it today?
2. **Today** is Monday.
3. Do we have a **calendar**?
4. Yes, it's over there.
5. Do you have a **schedule** for this **week**?
6. Yes, I do. Which **month** would you like to see?
7. **Next month**, please.
8. Alright. What appointments do we have **next month**?
9. We have two important meetings and one trip out of town.

✤ Thailand's traditional calendar was based on the Hindu cosmology and was officially replaced by the Gregorian calendar in 1888, yet the Buddhist Era year, 543 years ahead of the Gregorian calendar, is still widely used.

วันที่ 33: อาหาร I 🍴

1. วันนี้คุณอยากกินอะไร?
2. ฉันอยากกิน**ข้าว**กับ**เนื้อสัตว์**และผัก.
3. คุณอยากดื่มอะไร? ชา, กาแฟหรือเบียร์?
4. ฉันอยากดื่มชาร้อน.
5. หลังจากนั้นเรากิน**ขนมปัง**กับ**ไข่**ได้ไหม?
6. ได้สิ, และเรามี**ผลไม้**เป็นของหวาน.
7. ฉันชอบ**ผลไม้**เย็นๆ.
8. คุณชอบ**พาสต้า**ไหม?
9. ชอบ, แต่วันนี้ฉันอยากกิน**ข้าว**มากกว่า.

✤ In Thai, to form the passive voice for sentences about food, we often use the word "ถูก" (tùuk) before the verb to show that the action is being done to the subject.

1. Wannî khun xỳāk kin xarāi?
2. Chạn xỳāk kin **khāw** kạb **nūrasạtw̐** læa **phạk**.
3. Khun xỳāk dūm xarāi? **Chā, kāfæ rū̄ bia?**
4. Chạn xỳāk dūm **chā** r̂xn.
5. H̄lạngcāk nận rao kin **khnmpạng** kạb **khị̀** dị̂ mị̂?
6. Dị̂ s̄i, læa rao mī **phl mị̂** pěn k̄hngxwān.
7. Chạn chxb **phl mị̂** yen yen.
8. Khun chxb **phās̄t̂ā** mị̂?
9. Chxb, tæ̀ wạnnî chạn xỳāk kin **khāw** mākkwā.

DAY 33: FOOD I

1. What do you feel like eating today?
2. I feel like eating **rice** with **meat** and **vegetables**.
3. What would you like to drink? **Tea, coffee, or beer**?
4. I would like to drink hot **tea**.
5. After that, can we have **bread** with **eggs**?
6. Sure, and we have **fruit** for dessert.
7. I like cold **fruit**.
8. Do you like **pasta**?
9. Yes, but today I feel more like eating **rice**.

✤ In Thailand, the beloved dish Pad Thai was popularized during World War II to promote Thai nationalism and reduce rice consumption.

วันที่ 34: อาหาร ชุดที่ 2

1. วันนี้กินอาหารอะไรดี?
2. แซนด์วิชไก่หรือซุปเนื้อวัวดี?
3. แซนด์วิชไก่มีเนยและชีสด้วยไหม?
4. มีครับ และยังมีพริกไทยโรยหน้าด้วย
5. ดีจัง แล้วเรากินเค้กชาหรือกาแฟดี?
6. เค้กชากับกาแฟดูเข้ากันดีนะ
7. ใช่ แล้วเรากินสลัดหมูหรือเนื้อวัวดี?
8. สลัดหมูดีกว่า ผมชอบหมูมากกว่าเนื้อวัว
9. ตกลง แซนด์วิชไก่ กาแฟ และสลัดหมูนะ

✤ In Thai, to describe how someone eats a particular food, place the word for the food first, followed by "ด้วย" (duây) and then the method or utensil used.

1. Wannî kin **ʼāhār** ʼxrai dī?
2. **Sændwich** kị̀ h̄rụ̄x **s̄ūp** nụ̄awūa dī?
3. **Sændwich** kị̀ mī **neīy** læa **chīs** d̂wy h̄ịm?
4. Mī khrạb læa yang mī **phrikthịy** r̄xy n̂ā d̂wy
5. Dī cạng læaw ra kink **khek** chā h̄rụ̄x kāfæ dī?
6. **Khek** chā kạb kāfæ dū k̄hạn dī ná
7. Chî læaw ra kin **s̄ạld** mū h̄rụ̄x **nụ̄awūa** dī?
8. **S̄ạld** mū dī kwâ chạn chxb **mū** māk kwâ **nụ̄awūa**
9. Ṫxklng sændwich kị̀ kāfæ læa s̄ạld mū ná

1. What should we eat today?
2. Chicken **sandwich** or beef **soup**?
3. Does the chicken **sandwich** come with **butter** and **cheese**?
4. Yes, it does. And it also has **black pepper** sprinkled on top.
5. Great. Then should we have tea **cake** or coffee?
6. Tea **cake** with coffee sounds good.
7. Right. Should we have a pork **salad** or beef?
8. Pork **salad** is better. I prefer **pork** over **beef**.
9. Alright, chicken sandwich, coffee, and pork salad it is.

✤ In Thailand, the beloved dish Pad Thai was popularized during World War II to promote Thai nationalism and reduce rice consumption.

วันที่ 35: เครื่องดื่มและของหวาน ✑

1. วันนี้อยากดื่มน้ำผลไม้หรือ**โซดา**คะ?
2. ฉันอยากดื่ม**น้ำผลไม้**ครับ.
3. แล้วของหวานล่ะคะ? มี**ไอศกรีม, พาย, และขนมอบ.**
4. ฉันขอ**ไอศกรีม**กับ**ช็อคโกแลต**นะครับ.
5. ต้องการเพิ่ม**โทสต์**เนยด้วยไหมครับ?
6. ไม่เป็นไรครับ, ขอแค่**ไอศกรีม**กับ**ช็อคโกแลต**พอ.
7. ได้เลยครับ, รอสักครู่นะครับ.

✤ In Thai, an independent clause can stand alone as a sentence, like "ฉันชอบน้ำมะพร้าว" (I like coconut water), without needing another clause to make sense.

1. Wan nī̂ yāk dūem **nam phǫl māi** rēu **sō dā** kha?
2. Chǎn yāk dūem **nam phǫl māi** khrap.
3. Lǣo khǫ̌ng wān lā kha? Mī **'āi sōkrīm, phāi, lǣ khanom 'op.**
4. Chǎn khǫ̌ **'āi sōkrīm** kap **chôk kō lǣt** na khrap.
5. Tǒngkān phīm **thǫ st** noei dūai māi khrap?
6. Māi bpen rai khrap, khǫ̌ khae **'āi sōkrīm** kap **chôk kō lǣt** phǫ.
7. Dāi loei khrap, rō sàk khǔ na khrap.

1. Would you like to drink **fruit juice** or **soda** today?
2. I would like **fruit juice**, please.
3. And for dessert? We have **ice cream, pie, and baked goods**.
4. I'll have **ice cream** with **chocolate**, please.
5. Would you like to add **butter toast** as well?
6. No, thank you. Just the **ice cream** with **chocolate** is fine.
7. Right away, please wait a moment.

✤ In Thailand, the beloved dessert Mango Sticky Rice was traditionally made during the harvest season as a way to celebrate the bounty of fresh mangoes.

วันที่ 36: การทำอาหารและห้องครัว ✤

1. วันนี้เราจะ**อบ**อะไรดี?
2. ฉันอยาก**ย่าง**เนื้อสัตว์.
3. เราต้องใช้**เตาอบ**หรือไม่?
4. ใช่, และเตรียมจาน, **ส้อม, ช้อน**, และมีดด้วย.
5. เนื้อสัตว์อยู่ในตู้**เย็น**ไหม?
6. อยู่ตรงชั้นบนสุด. หลังจากนั้นเราจะทำ**ทอด**ผัก.
7. ดีมาก, ฉันจะเตรียมน้ำผลไม้และโซดา.
8. อย่าลืมเช็ค**ตู้เย็น**ว่ามีนมหรือเบียร์ไหม.
9. โอเค, หลังจากกินเราจะดูหนังกัน.

✤ In Thai, when describing how you cook something, the action you do first becomes the subordinate clause, like "Before I fry the chicken, I marinate it."

1. Wan nî ráo cà **òp** à-rai dī?
2. Chăn yàak **yâang** néua săt.
3. Ráo tông chái **tao òp** hrŭe mâi?
4. Châi, læa trīam **cān, sôm, chôn**, læa **mîd** dûai.
5. Néua săt yù thî **tû-yen** măi?
6. Yù trong chán bon sùt. Lăng cân nán ráo cà tham **thôt** phák.
7. Dī mâak, chăn cà trīam nám phọ-lá-mâi læa sō-dā.
8. Yà lŭem chék **tû-yen** wâa mī nom hrŭe biia măi.
9. Ō-kē, lăng cân kin ráo cà dū năng kan.

1. What should we **bake** today?
2. I want to **grill** some meat.
3. Do we need to use the **oven**?
4. Yes, and prepare **plates, forks, spoons**, and **knives** too.
5. Is the meat in the **fridge**?
6. It's on the very top shelf. After that, we'll **fry** some vegetables.
7. Great, I'll prepare some juice and soda.
8. Don't forget to check the **fridge** for milk or beer.
9. Okay, after eating we'll watch a movie.

✤ In Thailand, Chef McDang is revered not only for his culinary skills but also for elevating Thai cuisine on the global stage, making him a cultural ambassador through food.

วันที่ 37: การเดินทางและสถานที่ II

1. วันนี้เราจะไป**หาดทราย**กันไหม?
2. ฉันอยากไป**ภูเขา**มากกว่า
3. แต่ป่าใกล้**ภูเขา**น่าสนใจกว่า
4. เราสามารถผ่าน**แม่น้ำ**และ**ทะเล**ไป**เกาะ**ได้ไหม?
5. น่าสนใจนะ แต่ฉันกลัว**มหาสมุทร**
6. เราไป**หุบเขา**แล้วกลับมาที่**ทะเลทราย**ได้ไหม?
7. ฉันคิดว่าเราควรอยู่ใกล้**ดงดิบ**มากกว่า
8. ใช่ แล้วเราจะได้เห็น**ฤดูร้อน**ที่สวยงาม
9. ดีมาก ครอบครัวของเราจะชอบแน่นอน

✤ In Thai, to form a complex sentence about travel, you can use the conjunction "และ" (láe) meaning "and" or "แต่" (tàe) meaning "but" to connect two simple sentences, like "I want to go to Bangkok, but it is raining."

1. Wannī rao cà pāi **hāt sāi** kan mǎi?
2. Chǎn xỳàk pāi **phū khǎo** māk kwà
3. Tæ̀ **pà** klai **phū khǎo** nâ sǎnīng kwà
4. Rao sǎmāt phàn **mæ̀ nám** læ **thalē** pāi **kò** dâi mǎi?
5. Nâ sǎnīng ná, tæ̀ chǎn klūa **mahǎsǎmùt**
6. Rao pāi **hùp khǎo** læ̀ klạp mā thī **thalē sāi** dâi mǎi?
7. Chǎn khít wâ rao khūan yù klai **dong dìp** māk kwà
8. Châi, læ̀ rao cà dâi hěn **rǔdū rón** thī sūay ngām
9. Dī māk, khrǎpkhrūa khǎng rao cà chǎp nǎenǒn

1. Are we going to the **beach** today?
2. I'd rather go to the **mountains**.
3. But the **forest** near the **mountains** is more interesting.
4. Can we pass through the **river** and the **sea** to get to the **island**?
5. That sounds interesting, but I'm afraid of the **ocean**.
6. Can we go to the **valley** and then return to the **desert**?
7. I think we should stay closer to the **wilderness**.
8. Yes, then we can see the beautiful **summer**.
9. Great, our family will definitely like it.

✤ In Thailand, the legendary traveler Jim Thompson revitalized the Thai silk industry before mysteriously disappearing in the Malaysian jungle.

วันที่ 38: ฉุกเฉินและสุขภาพ

1. ฉันแพ้น้ำผลไม้ค่ะ
2. คุณต้องการช่วยเหลือไหมครับ?
3. ใช่ค่ะ, ฉันรู้สึกไม่ดี
4. เราควรโทรหาตำรวจหรือไปโรงพยาบาลดีครับ?
5. ไปโรงพยาบาลดีกว่าค่ะ, ฉันต้องการพบแพทย์
6. คุณมีบาดแผลไหมครับ?
7. ไม่ค่ะ, แต่ฉันรู้สึกแย่มาก
8. โอเคครับ, ฉันจะหายาและเม็ดยาให้คุณ
9. ขอบคุณมากค่ะ, คุณช่วยฉันได้มากเลย

✤ In Thai, words related to emergencies and health do not change form based on gender; instead, context and pronouns indicate the gender of the person involved.

1. chạn **phǽ** nám phól maị khạ
2. khun tôngkān **chûay heǔa** hịm khrạb?
3. chị khạ, chạn rû sùk mị dī
4. rāw khwr tho hǎ **tạmrwc** hrụx bpai **rōng phạyābāl** dī khrạb?
5. bpai **rōng phạyābāl** dī kwà khạ, chạn îxngkān phb **phǽtỷ**
6. khun mī **bād phlǽ** hịm khrạb?
7. mị khạ, tæ̀ chạn rû sùk yæ̀ māk
8. xokh khrạb, chạn ōhā hǎ **yā** læa **med yā** hị khun
9. khxbkhuṇ māk khạ, khun chûay chạn dị māk leǔxy

1. I'm **allergic** to fruit juice.
2. Do you need **help**?
3. Yes, I'm feeling unwell.
4. Should we call the **police** or go to the **hospital**?
5. Going to the **hospital** is better, I need to see a **doctor**.
6. Do you have any **injuries**?
7. No, but I feel very bad.
8. Okay, I'll find some **medicine** and **pills** for you.
9. Thank you so much, you've been a great help.

✤ In Thailand, traditional Thai massage, recognized by UNESCO, is an integral part of the country's healthcare system, blending healing techniques that have been passed down for centuries.

1. ฉันมี **ยี่สิบเอ็ด** จาน แต่ต้องการ **ยี่สิบสอง** จาน คุณมีจาน
เพิ่มไหม?

2. มีครับ แต่ฉันมี **ยี่สิบสาม** ส้อม และ **ยี่สิบสี่** ช้อนเท่านั้น

3. ไม่เป็นไรค่ะ ฉันมี **ยี่สิบห้า** ช้อนอยู่แล้ว

4. ดีมากครับ แล้วเรามี **ยี่สิบหก** แก้วน้ำหรือยัง?

5. ฉันมี **ยี่สิบเจ็ด** แก้วค่ะ แต่ฉันกลัวว่ามันจะไม่พอ

6. ฉันจะไปหาเพิ่มให้ ฉันคิดว่าโรงพยาบาลใกล้ๆ นี้มี **ยี่สิบ
แปด** แก้ว

7. โรงพยาบาลหรือคะ? ทำไมไม่ไปร้านค้าล่ะคะ?

8. อ๋อ ฉันสับสน ฉันหมายถึงร้านค้าที่มี **ยี่สิบเก้า** แก้วน้ำ

9. โอเคค่ะ แล้วเราจะมี **สามสิบ** แก้วน้ำพอดีเลย!

✤ In Thai, numbers 21-29 are formed by saying "twenty" (ยี่สิบ yîi sìp) followed by the
number 1-9, but for 20, just say "twenty" (ยี่สิบ yîi sìp) without adding a number after.

1. chạn mī **yīsibed** cān tæ̀ dị̂xngkār **yīsibs̄xng** cān khun mī cān phìm h̄ịm?

2. mī khrạb tæ̀ chạn mī **yīsibs̄ām** s̄̂xm læ **yīsibs̄ī̀** ch̀n thậnxn

3. mị̀ pĕn rị kạ̄ chạn mī **yīsibh̄̂ā** ch̀n xyū̀ læ̂w

4. dī māk khrạb læ̂w rao mī **yīsibh̄k** kæ̂wnạm h̄rụ̄x yạng?

5. chạn mī **yīsibcĕd** kæ̂w kạ̄ tæ̀ chạn klụ̄a wā man cā phx

6. chạn cā pị h̄ā phìm h̄ị̂ chạn khid wā rong phạyābāl kịl̂xxy nī̂ mī **yīsibpæd**
kæ̂w

7. rong phạyābāl h̄rụ̄x kạ? thảmịy mị̀ pị r̂ān kĥā là kạ?

8. xx chạn s̄ạb s̄n chạn h̄māy t̄hụng r̂ān kĥā thī̀ mī **yīsibkāw** kæ̂wnạm

9. xokhê kạ læ̂w rao cā mī **s̄āms̄ib** kæ̂wnạm phxdī lxy!

1. I have **twenty-one** plates, but I need **twenty-two** plates. Do you have any more plates?
2. Yes, I do. But I only have **twenty-three** forks and **twenty-four** spoons.
3. That's okay, I already have **twenty-five** spoons.
4. Great! Do we have **twenty-six** glasses yet?
5. I have **twenty-seven** glasses, but I'm afraid that might not be enough.
6. I'll go find some more. I think the hospital nearby has **twenty-eight** glasses.
7. The hospital? Why not go to a store?
8. Oh, I got confused. I meant the store that has **twenty-nine** glasses.
9. Okay, then we will have exactly **thirty** glasses!

✚ In Thailand, people often interpret dreams or unusual events as signs for choosing lottery numbers.

วันที่ 40: วันในสัปดาห์

1. เมื่อวานคุณทำอะไร
2. เมื่อวานผมไปหาดทราย.
3. วันนี้ล่ะ?
4. วันนี้ผมจะไปป่า.
5. พรุ่งนี้คุณมีแผนอะไร?
6. พรุ่งนี้ผมคิดจะไปภูเขา.
7. คุณชอบวันเสาร์หรือวันอาทิตย์มากกว่ากัน?
8. ผมชอบวันเสาร์เพราะผมสามารถพักผ่อนได้.
9. ดีมาก, สนุกกับการเดินทางนะ.

✤ In Thai, to compare days of the week, we often use "กว่า" (gwàa) for "more than" and "น้อยกว่า" (nɔ́ɔi gwàa) for "less than," as in "วันเสาร์มีคนมากกว่าวันอาทิตย์" (Saturday has more people than Sunday).

1. **Mửa wān** khun tham arai
2. Mửa wān phŏm pai **hāt sāi**.
3. **Wan nî** lè?
4. Wan nî phŏm ca pai **pà**.
5. **Phrung nî** khun mī phăen arai?
6. Phrung nî phŏm khit ca pai **phū khǎo**.
7. Khun chŏp **wan sāo** rū wan ʻāthitỷ māk kwà khan?
8. Phŏm chŏp **wan sāo** phrǎ phŏm sāmākan phak phŏn dāi.
9. Dī māk, sanuk kap kān doēn thāng ná.

DAY 40: DAYS OF THE WEEK

1. **Yesterday** what did you do?
2. Yesterday I went to the **beach**.
3. **What about today?**
4. Today I'm going to the **forest**.
5. **What are your plans for tomorrow?**
6. Tomorrow I plan to go to the **mountains**.
7. Do you prefer **Saturday** or **Sunday**?
8. I prefer **Saturday** because I can relax.
9. Great, enjoy your trip.

✤ In Thailand, it's believed that each day of the week is governed by a specific god and color, influencing one's luck and life events.

CHALLENGE NO. 4

WRITE A LETTER OR EMAIL IN THAI TO A FICTIONAL OR REAL FRIEND.

พัฒนาตนเองไม่มีที่สิ้นสุด

Self-improvement is endless.

วันที่ 41: ทำความสะอาด I ✦

1. วันนี้เราจะทำความสะอาดห้องนั่งเล่นกันนะ
2. ใช่ ฉันจะเริ่มจากโซฟา
3. ดีมาก แล้วฉันจะทำความสะอาดโต๊ะและเก้าอี้
4. เยี่ยม หลังจากนั้นเรามาทำความสะอาดห้องน้ำ
5. แล้วห้องครัวล่ะ?
6. ฉันจะทำห้องครัว อย่าลืมโคมไฟและประตูนะ
7. แน่นอน แล้วเราจะทำความสะอาดหน้าต่างและผนังด้วย
8. ทำงานร่วมกัน บ้านเราจะสะอาดแน่นอน
9. ใช่ ทำความสะอาดบ้านด้วยกันมันก็สนุกดีนะ

✤ In Thai, to form the superlative, you often use "ที่สุด" (tîi sùt) after an adjective, meaning "the most."

1. Nî nî rāo cà tham khwām s̄ā'ād h̄xng nạnglen kan ná
2. Chı̣ chan cà rìm càk sôfā
3. Dī māk lǣw chan cà tham khwām s̄ā'ād tô lǣa kô'ī
4. Yîm lǣngcàk nán rāo mā tham khwām s̄ā'ād h̄xng n̂ām
5. Lǣw h̄xng khruā lā?
6. Chan cà tham h̄xng khruā yà lỳm khom lị fǣ lǣa prtū ná
7. Nǣn xn lǣw rāo cà tham khwām s̄ā'ād n̂ā tâ h̄xng lǣa phnạng dūay
8. Tham ngān r̀wm kan bān rāo cà s̄ā'ād nǣn xn
9. Chı̣ tham khwām s̄ā'ād bān dūay kan man k̄h̄x s̄nuk dī ná

1. Today, we're going to **clean** the living room together.
2. Right, I'll start with the **sofa**.
3. Great, then I'll clean the **table** and **chairs**.
4. Excellent, after that, let's clean the **bathroom**.
5. What about the **kitchen**?
6. I'll take care of the **kitchen**. Don't forget the **lamps** and **doors**.
7. Of course, then we'll clean the **windows** and **walls** as well.
8. Working together, our house will definitely be clean.
9. Yes, cleaning the house together is actually quite fun.

✤ In Thailand, the annual Songkran festival transforms the act of cleaning into a nationwide water fight, symbolizing the washing away of bad luck and misfortunes.

วันที่ 42: ทำความสะอาด 2

1. วันนี้เราต้องทำความสะอาด**บ้านหรืออพาร์ตเมนต์**กันแล้วนะ
2. ใช่, เริ่มจาก**หลังคาหรือระเบียง**ก่อนดี?
3. ฉันคิดว่าเราควรเริ่มจาก**ห้องและสวน**ก่อน
4. แล้ว**โรงรถ**ล่ะ?
5. เราจะทำความสะอาด**โรงรถ**หลังจาก**บันไดและพื้น**
6. อย่าลืม**เพดาน**ด้วยนะ
7. ใช่, และเราต้องทำความสะอาด**โซฟา, โต๊ะ, เก้าอี้และเตียง**ด้วย
8. **ห้องน้ำ**ต้องทำความสะอาดทุกวัน
9. ดีมาก, เราจะทำให้ทุกอย่างสะอาดเรียบร้อย

✤ In Thai, to compare two things, we often use "กว่า" (more than) after the adjective.

1. Wan nî ráo tông tham khwam sà àat **bâan** rěu **'a phā rt men** kan láeo ná
2. Châi, rêm càak **hlǎng kā** rěu **ra bēing** gòn dî?
3. Chǎn khit wâa ráo khuǎn rêm càak **hông** láe **suan** gòn
4. Láeo **rōng ròt** lâ?
5. Ráo cà tham khwam sà àat **rōng ròt** lǎng càak **ban dai** láe **phūn**
6. Yà leum **phē dan** dûay ná
7. Châi, láe ráo tông tham khwam sà àat **sō fā, tó, kâo î** láe **tiang** dûay
8. **Hông nâm** tông tham khwam sà àat thuk wan
9. Dî mâak, ráo cà tham hâi thuk yàang sà àat rîap rói

1. Today, we need to clean the **house** or **apartment**.
2. Right, should we start with the **roof** or **balcony** first?
3. I think we should start with the **rooms** and **garden** first.
4. What about the **garage**?
5. We'll clean the **garage** after the **stairs** and **floor**.
6. Don't forget the **ceiling** too.
7. Yes, and we need to clean the **sofa, table, chairs**, and **bed** as well.
8. The **bathroom** needs to be cleaned every day.
9. Great, we'll make everything clean and tidy.

✤ In Thailand, the invention of the electric rice cooker revolutionized kitchens, turning a complex, time-consuming task into a simple, everyday convenience.

วันที่ 43: ทิศทางและตำแหน่ง II

1. **ที่นี่** สวนหรือไม่?
2. ไม่ใช่, **ที่นั่น** สวน.
3. ห้องของเราอยู่ **บน** หรือ **ล่าง**?
4. อยู่ **บน** หลังคา.
5. เราจะไปสถานีรถไฟ **ข้างหลัง** อพาร์ตเมนต์ได้ไหม?
6. ได้, แต่ต้องเดินผ่านสวน **ระหว่าง** อพาร์ตเมนต์.
7. เราจะดื่มอะไร? **ชา, กาแฟ, หรือ เบียร์?**
8. ฉันอยากดื่ม **ชา**.
9. โอเค, เราจะนั่ง **ข้างๆ** หรือ **ข้างใน**?
10. **ข้างใน** ดีกว่า, มีแอร์.

✤ In Thai, to indicate direction or location, place the verb before the preposition and then the location word.

1. thì nî̌ s̄wn h̄rụ̄x mị̀?
2. mị̀ chì, thì nận s̄wn.
3. h̄̂xng k̄hxng reā xỳū thì bn h̄rụ̄x l̀āng?
4. xỳū bn h̄lạngkhā.
5. reā cā pị s̄t̄hānī rthfị k̄ĥāngh̄lạng xphār̥tmen dị̀ mị̀?
6. dị̀, tæ̀ t̂xng dern p̄h̀ān s̄wn r̥ah̄ẁāng xphār̥tmen.
7. reā cā deūm xarị? chā, kāfæ, h̄rụ̄x bīer?
8. c̄hạn xyāk deūm chā.
9. xokh, reā cā nạng k̄ĥāngkhị h̄rụ̄x k̄ĥāngnı?
10. k̄ĥāngnı dī kwa, mī xær.

134

1. Is this a garden?
2. No, the garden is over there.
3. Is our room upstairs or downstairs?
4. It's upstairs, on the roof.
5. Can we go to the train station behind the apartment?
6. Yes, but we have to walk through the garden between the apartments.
7. What shall we drink? Tea, coffee, or beer?
8. I'd like some tea.
9. Okay, shall we sit outside or inside?
10. Inside is better, there's air conditioning.

✦ In Thailand, the city of Bangkok was so intricately planned that its full ceremonial name is considered the world's longest place name, mapping out its glory and spiritual centers.

วันที่ 44: ช้อปปิ้ง ครั้งที่ 3 ✎

1. วันนี้เราจะไป**ศูนย์การค้า**กันไหม?
2. ดีมาก, ฉันอยากไป**ซูเปอร์มาร์เก็ต**ด้วย.
3. เราต้องการ**ตะกร้า**หนึ่งใบสำหรับของที่เราจะซื้อ.
4. ใช่, และอย่าลืมเช็ค**ราคา**และ**ส่วนลด**ด้วยนะ.
5. หลังจากซื้อของเสร็จ เราต้องไปที่**เคาน์เตอร์จ่ายเงิน**.
6. ถ้ามีปัญหา เราสามารถขอ**การคืนเงิน**ได้ไหม?
7. ได้, แต่ต้องมี**ใบเสร็จ**เสมอ.
8. หวังว่าเราจะได้ของที่**ลดราคา**เยอะๆ.
9. ใช่, ฉันก็หวังเช่นกัน.

✤ In Thai, when asking a question about shopping, the verb often comes before the subject, like "Buy what?" instead of "What buy?"

1. Wannī rao cà pāi **sūnyā kān khā** kan mị?

2. Dī māk, chan yàk pāi **sû per mār kēt** dûai.

3. Rao t̄xngkān **takrā** nụ̄ng bai samrạb k̄hxng thī rao cà sū̄.

4. Chị, læa xỳā lūm chek **rākhā** læa s̀wn lōd dûai ná.

5. L̄ngcāk sū̄ k̄hxng s̄r̂c, rao t̄xng pāi thī **khān t̂xr cāy ngein**.

6. T̄hā mī pạṇhā, rao s̄āmārt k̄hx̀ **kār khụ̄n ngein** dị mị?

7. Dị, tæ̀ t̄xng mī **bı s̄r̂c** s̄emụ̄x.

8. H̄wạng wā rao cā dị k̄hxng thī **lōd rākhā** yeụ̄x.

9. Chị, chan k̄h̀ h̄wạng chen kan.

1. Are we going to the **shopping center** today?
2. Great, I want to go to the **supermarket** too.
3. We need one **basket** for the things we're going to buy.
4. Yes, and don't forget to check the **prices** and **discounts**.
5. After shopping, we need to go to the **checkout counter**.
6. If there's a problem, can we ask for a **refund**?
7. Yes, but you always need a **receipt**.
8. Hope we find a lot of **discounted** items.
9. Yes, I hope so too.

✤ In Thailand, gifts are traditionally given with the right hand, symbolizing respect and good intentions.

วันที่ 45: เงินและการชำระเงิน 🌱

1. ฉันอยากซื้อโซดาที่ซูเปอร์มาร์เก็ต
2. คุณมีเงินสดหรือจะใช้บัตรเครดิต?
3. ฉันมีแต่เหรียญกับธนบัตรเอง
4. ไม่เป็นไรครับ ที่นี่รับเงินสดทุกสกุลเงิน
5. อัตราแลกเปลี่ยนเป็นอย่างไรบ้างคะ?
6. วันนี้อัตราแลกเปลี่ยนดีมากครับ คุณสามารถเช็คที่
   เอทีเอ็มได้
7. ขอบคุณค่ะ แล้วฉันจะใช้บัตรเดบิตจ่ายที่เคาน์เตอร์จ่ายเงิน
8. ได้เลยครับ หลังจากนั้นอย่าลืมเก็บเงินสดทอนและเหรียญ
   ด้วยนะครับ
9. ขอบคุณมากค่ะ

✤ In Thai, the amount of money comes before the currency when talking about prices, like "100 baht" not "baht 100."

1. chạn yāk **sự** sōdā thī sūpeo mākēt
2. khun mī **ngoen sọt** rử chā chái **bat krēdit**?
3. chạn mī tæ̀ **rīan** kàp **than bat** œng
4. mị̀ pen rai khráp thī nî̂ rap **ngoen sọt** thuk **sakun ngoen**
5. **atrā læ kplīan** pen yāng rai bāng khá?
6. wan nî̂ **atrā læ kplīan** dī māk khráp khun sāmārt chěk thī **ētīēm** dị̂
7. kh̀xbkhuṇ khà læw chạn chā chái **bat debit** chái thī **khaūn tœ̈r chāi ngoen**
8. dị̂ leiy khráp h̄lạngcāk nạn yà lụm kheb **ngoen sọt** thon læa **rīan** dūay ná khráp
9. kh̀xbkhuṇ māk khà

138

1. I want to **buy** soda at the supermarket.
2. Do you have **cash** or will you use a **credit card**?
3. I only have **coins** and **banknotes**.
4. No problem, sir. We accept **cash** in all **currencies**.
5. How is the **exchange rate**?
6. The **exchange rate** is very good today, ma'am. You can check at the **ATM**.
7. Thank you. Then I will use my **debit card** to pay at the **checkout counter**.
8. Certainly, sir. After that, don't forget to collect your **cash** change and **coins**.
9. Thank you very much.

♣ In ancient Thailand, bullet coins were used as currency, uniquely shaped like bullets rather than the flat coins we use today.

วันที่ 46: เวลาและธรรมชาติ 🌱

1. วันนี้อากาศอย่างไรบ้าง?
2. **พยากรณ์**บอกว่าจะมี**เสียงฟ้าร้องและฟ้าผ่า**ครับ.
3. แล้วจะมี**ฝนปรอยๆ**หรือเปล่า?
4. ใช่ครับ, แต่หลังจากนั้น**แดดจ้า**จะออก.
5. ฟังดูจะ**ชื้น**มากเลยนะ.
6. ใช่ค่ะ, แต่เราอาจจะเห็น**รุ้ง**หลังฝนหยุด.
7. มองเห็น**เมฆ**ไหม?
8. ตอนนี้เห็น**เมฆ**เยอะมากค่ะ.
9. สวยจังเลยนะ.

✤ In Thai, to form weather-related words, often add "nám" (water) for rain-related terms and "lôm" (wind) for wind-related terms.

1. wan nī **ākās** yāng rai bāng?
2. **phayākǫn** bøk wā cā mī **sīang fā rǫng** læ **fā phā** khrap.
3. læa cā mī **fǒn próy próy** h̄rǔx bplào?
4. chì khrap, tæ̀ h̄lạng cāk nán **dæd c̄hā** cā x̀k.
5. fang dū cā **chụ̄n** māk lēi ná.
6. chì khà, tæ̀ rao xāc cā h̄ěn **rûng** h̄lạng fǒn h̄yud.
7. mǒng h̄ěn **mekh** mǐ?
8. tawnî h̄ěn **mekh** yeǔx māk khà.
9. s̄wy cạng lēi ná.

1. How's the **weather** today?
2. The **forecast** says there will be **thunder** and **lightning**.
3. Will there be any **light rain**?
4. Yes, but after that, the **sun will shine**.
5. Sounds like it's going to be very **humid**.
6. Yes, but we might see a **rainbow** after the rain stops.
7. Can you see any **clouds**?
8. Right now, there are a lot of **clouds**.
9. That sounds beautiful.

✤ In Thai mythology, the Himmapan Forest is a legendary realm filled with mythical creatures and magical plants, believed to exist in the Himalayas.

1. **พายุเฮอริเคน** กำลังมา, ฟ้าผ่าศูนย์การค้า.
2. ใช่, ฉันได้ยิน **เสียงฟ้าร้อง** เมื่อคืน.
3. คุณคิดว่าจะมี **แผ่นดินไหว** ไหม?
4. ไม่แน่นอน, แต่ **พายุทอร์นาโด** ก็เป็นไปได้.
5. ฉันหวังว่า **ภูเขาไฟ** ใกล้ **หุบเขา** จะไม่ระเบิด.
6. เราควรซื้อของที่ **ร้านขายของชำ** และเตรียม **ตะกร้า**.
7. ใช่, ไปที่ **เคาน์เตอร์จ่ายเงิน** ก่อนที่อากาศจะ **ร้อน** มาก.
8. หลังจากนั้นเราไปหาที่พักที่ **ทะเลสงบ** หรือ ป่า ดี?
9. ป่า ดีกว่า, มันจะ **เย็น** และ **ชื้น**.

✤ In Thai, the tone of a word can change its meaning, so it's important to practice the correct tone when talking about disasters and geography to avoid misunderstandings.

1. **Phāyuhērikhen** kamlang mā, fā phā sūn kār khā.
2. Chāi, chan dāi yin **sīang fā rǫng** meūa kheun.
3. Khun khid wā cā mī **phæn din wāi** māi?
4. Mai nænǫn, tæ **phāyuthǫnādō** kǫ pen pai dāi.
5. Chan wang wā **phūkhao fai** klai **hup khao** cā māi rabēt.
6. Rao khuan sū khǫng thī **rān khāi khǫng cham** læa triēm **takrā**.
7. Chāi, pai thī **khāun tēo cāi ngoen** kǫn thī ākāt cā **rǫn** māk.
8. Langcāknān rao pai hā thī phak thī **thalē sāngop** rŭ **pā** dī?
9. **Pā** dī kwa, man cā **yen** læa **chuen**.

1. **Hurricane** is coming, lightning strikes the shopping center.
2. Yes, I heard **thunder** last night.
3. Do you think there will be an **earthquake**?
4. Not sure, but a **tornado** is also possible.
5. I hope the **volcano** near the **valley** doesn't erupt.
6. We should buy supplies at the **grocery store** and prepare a **basket**.
7. Yes, let's go to the **checkout counter** before it gets too **hot**.
8. After that, should we find shelter at the **calm sea** or in the **forest**?
9. The **forest** is better, it will be **cool** and **humid**.

✤ In Thai legend, earthquakes are the result of the mythical giant fish, Phaya Naga, moving its massive body in the depths of the ocean.

วันที่ 48: สี 🖌

1. สีที่ชอบคืออะไร?
2. ฉันชอบสี**เขียว**.
3. แล้วสีที่ไม่ชอบล่ะ?
4. ฉันไม่ชอบสีดำเท่าไหร่.
5. ทำไมล่ะ?
6. เพราะมันทำให้ฉันรู้สึกเศร้า.
7. ฉันเข้าใจแล้ว. ฉันชอบสีน้ำเงิน.
8. สีน้ำเงินสวยดีนะ.
9. ใช่, มันทำให้ฉันรู้สึกสงบ.

✤ In Thai, the tone of a word can change its meaning, so when saying colors, make sure to use the correct tone to avoid confusion.

1. sǐ thǐ chǒp khŭx aray?
2. chạn chǒp sī **khīaw**.
3. lǽo sǐ thǐ mị̀ chǒp lạ?
4. chạn mị̀ chǒp sī **dam** thả h̄rị̀.
5. thamai lạ?
6. phrā mạn tham h̄ị̀ chạn rū̂ s̄ùk ṣ̄ærā.
7. chạn khâo cî lǽw. chạn chǒp sī **ńángīn**.
8. sī **ńángīn** s̄wy dī nạ.
9. chî, man tham h̄ị̀ chạn rū̂ s̄ùk s̄ngb.

1. What's your favorite color?
2. I like **green**.
3. What about the color you don't like?
4. I don't really like **black**.
5. Why is that?
6. Because it makes me feel sad.
7. I see. I like **blue**.
8. **Blue** is pretty nice.
9. Yes, it makes me feel calm.

✤ In Thailand, the Songkran Festival transforms the streets into vibrant spectacles of water fights, symbolizing purification and the washing away of sins, all amidst a kaleidoscope of colorful traditional outfits and decorations.

วันที่ 49: เทคโนโลยี I

1. ฉันควรใช้ **อินเทอร์เน็ต** บน **สมาร์ทโฟน** หรือ **คอมพิวเตอร์** ดี?
2. ถ้าอยู่นอกบ้าน, ใช้ **สมาร์ทโฟน** สะดวกกว่า. แต่ถ้าทำงาน, **คอมพิวเตอร์** หรือ **แล็ปท็อป** ดีกว่า.
3. ฉันชอบส่ง **อีเมล** ผ่าน **แล็ปท็อป**. แต่ต้องเชื่อมต่อ **ไวไฟ** ก่อน.
4. ใช่, และฉันชอบเล่น **โซเชียลเน็ตเวิร์ก** บน **สมาร์ทโฟน**.
5. ฉันต้องการ **ดาวน์โหลด แอปพลิเคชัน** ใหม่. แนะนำใช้ **เบราว์เซอร์** อะไร?
6. ลองใช้ Google Chrome หรือ Safari.

✤ In Thai, when talking about technology, the stress often falls on the final syllable of the word.

1. chạn khwr chî **inthexrnet** bn **smārthofn** ห̄rụ̄x **khxmphiwtețr** dī?
2. thả xỳ nxxk b̂ān, chî **smārthofn** s̄ādwk k̀wā. tæ̀ thả thảngān, **khxmphiwtețr** ห̄rụ̄x **læpthxph** dī k̀wā.
3. chạn chxb s̄̀ng **īmel** p̄hæn **læpthxph**. tæ̀ t̂xng cheụ̄̀xmt̀x **wị wị** k̀xn.
4. chî, læa chạn chxb len **socheị̄ynetweȓk** bn **smārthofn**.
5. chạn t̂xngkār **dāwṅhlod æphphlikhechạn** mị̀. næanảm chî **beroạwseȓ** àrị?
6. lxng chî Google Chrome ห̄rụ̄x Safari.

146

1. Should I use **internet** on a **smartphone** or a **computer**?
2. If you're outside, using a **smartphone** is more convenient. But for work, a **computer** or **laptop** is better.
3. I prefer to send **emails** through a **laptop**. But I need to connect to **Wi-Fi** first.
4. Yes, and I like to use **social networks** on a **smartphone**.
5. I need to **download** a new **application**. Which **browser** should I use?
6. Try using Google Chrome or Safari.

♣ In Thailand, the world's first non-English newspaper, the Bangkok Recorder, was launched in 1844 by an American missionary.

วันที่ 50: เทคโนโลยี II

1. วันนี้ วันอะไร?
2. วันพุธครับ.
3. คุณดูข่าวบนโทรทัศน์หรือวิทยุ?
4. ผมดูบนโทรทัศน์ครับ แต่ใช้รีโมทหาช่องไม่เจอ.
5. คุณลองตรวจสอบรหัสผ่านของอินเทอร์เน็ตหรือยัง?
6. ยังครับ, ผมลืมชื่อผู้ใช้และรหัสผ่าน.
7. ถ้างั้น ลองส่งอีเมลขอความช่วยเหลือไหม?
8. ดีครับ, ผมจะใช้คอมพิวเตอร์ส่งเลย.
9. อย่าลืมตรวจสอบหน้าจอและเครื่องพิมพ์นะครับ อาจจะ
   ต้องพิมพ์ข้อมูล.

✤ In Thai, words related to technology often borrow English terms, so remember, they don't carry the traditional Thai tones.

1. **wan nî** wan à-rai?
2. wan phūt khráp.
3. khun du **khào** bon **thō-rá-thát** rǔe **wít-thá-yú**?
4. phǒm du bon **thō-rá-thát** khráp tàe chái **rī-mọt** hǎ **chǒng** mâi jeū.
5. khun lǒng trūat sǒp **rá-hàt-sàn** khǒng **in-thē-net** rǔe yang?
6. yang khráp, phǒm lǔem **chû-phû-chái** læ **rá-hàt-sàn**.
7. thâ-ngán, lǒng sòng **ī-mel** khǒ khwām chūai hělūa mǎi?
8. dī khráp, phǒm jà chái **khǒm-phíu-thêet** sòng loei.
9. yà lǔem trūat sǒp **nà jǒ** læ **khrêuang phim** ná khráp, à-jà jà tǒng phim khǒ-mun.

1. **What day is it today?**
2. It's Wednesday.
3. Do you watch the **news** on **television** or **radio**?
4. I watch it on **television**, but I can't find the **channel** with the **remote**.
5. Have you checked the **internet password** yet?
6. Not yet, I forgot the **username** and **password**.
7. In that case, how about sending an **email** asking for help?
8. Good idea, I'll use the **computer** to send it right away.
9. Don't forget to check the **screen** and **printer**, you might need to print the information.

✤ In Thailand, a beauty queen's impactful tweet once sparked a nationwide conversation on democracy, showcasing the power of social media in shaping public discourse.

CHALLENGE NO. 5

LISTEN TO A PODCAST IN THAI AND SUMMARIZE IT, IN WRITING OR ORALLY.

ความอยากรู้เป็นประตูสู่ความรู้
Curiosity is the door to knowledge.

วันที่ 51: สัตว์ 🦜

1. คุณชอบสัตว์ชนิดไหน?
2. ฉันชอบนกและปลา.
3. แล้วคุณล่ะ?
4. ฉันชอบแมวกับหมามาก.
5. คุณมีม้าหรือวัวที่บ้านไหม?
6. ไม่มีเลย, แต่ฉันมีหมูสองตัว.
7. สนุกไหม?
8. ใช่, แต่ต้องดูแลหมูและไก่ด้วย.

✤ In Thai, to link a noun like "cat" (แมว - maeo) with an adjective like "small" (เล็ก - lek), we simply put the adjective after the noun, so "small cat" is "แมวเล็ก" (maeo lek).

1. khun chxb **sat** chnid h̄i?
2. c̄hạn chxb **nk̄h** læa **plā**.
3. læa khun l̀ā?
4. c̄hạn chxb **mæw** kạb **mā** māk.
5. khun mī **mā** h̄rụ̄x **wūa** thī̀ b̂ān h̄ịm?
6. mị̀ mī leīy, tæ̀ c̄hạn mī **mū** s̄xng tūa.
7. snuk h̄ịm?
8. chı̂, tæ̀ t̂xng dū læ **mū** læa **kị̀** d̂ūy.

152

1. What kind of **animals** do you like?
2. I like **birds** and **fish**.
3. What about you?
4. I really like **cats** and **dogs**.
5. Do you have any **horses** or **cows** at home?
6. Not at all, but I have two **pigs**.
7. Is it fun?
8. Yes, but I have to take care of the **pigs** and **chickens** too.

✤ In Thailand, the mythical Garuda, a bird-like creature, symbolizes the authority of the king and is a national emblem.

วันที่ 52: พืชและธรรมชาติ ✎

1. วันนี้เราจะไปป่าไหม?
2. อยากไปดู**ต้นไม้**และ**ดอกไม้**ในป่าดงดิบมากๆ
3. ใช่, และเราอาจจะเห็นนกกับ**ปลา**ในแม่น้ำด้วย
4. ฉันหวังว่าจะเห็น**หญ้า**และ**ใบไม้สวยๆ** ทำให้รู้สึกผ่อนคลาย
5. หลังจากนั้นเราจะไป**ภูเขา**หรือมหาสมุทรไหม?
6. ไป**ภูเขา**ดีกว่า ฉันอยากอยู่กับธรรมชาติและรู้สึกร่าเริง
7. ตกลง, วันนี้จะเป็นวันที่ดีที่สุดในการสัมผัสกับ**พืช**และ
   ธรรมชาติ
8. ใช่, ฉันรู้สึก**สุข**ใจที่ได้ออกไปข้างนอกและห่างไกล
   จากอินเทอร์เน็ต
9. วันนี้จะเป็นวันที่ดีที่สุด!

✤ In Thai, when talking about plants and nature, we often drop the final sound of a word to make the sentence flow more smoothly, like turning "dâk mái" (to pick flowers) into "dâk mâi".

1. Wannî rao cà pāi **pà** mǎi?
2. Yàk pai du **tôn mái** læ **dòk mái** nai **pà dong dip** mâk mâk
3. Châi, læ rao ǎt cà hěn **nók** kàp **plā** nai **mê nám** dûai
4. Chǎn wǎng wâ cà hěn **yâ** læ **bai mái** sǔai sǔai tham hâi rú sùk **ph̀xn klai**
5. Lǎng càk nán rao cà pai **phū khǎo** rǔ **mahǎ sàmùt** mǎi?
6. Pai **phū khǎo** dī kwa chǎn yàk yù kàp thammachāt læ rú sùk **râ reng**
7. Tòk long, wannî cà pěn wan thî dī thî sùt nai kān sàm phàt kàp **phûet** læ
   thammachāt
8. Châi, chǎn rú sùk **sùk jai** thî dâi òk pai khǎng nòk læ hǎng klai càk inthēnet
9. Wannî cà pěn wan thî dī thî sùt!

154

DAY 52: PLANTS AND NATURE

1. Are we going to the **forest** today?
2. I really want to see the **trees** and **flowers** in the **dense forest**.
3. Yes, and we might see **birds** and **fish** in the **river** too.
4. I hope to see beautiful **grass** and **leaves** that make me feel **relaxed**.
5. After that, shall we go to the **mountains** or the **ocean**?
6. Let's go to the **mountains**; I want to be with nature and feel **joyful**.
7. Alright, today will be the best day to connect with **plants** and nature.
8. Yes, I feel **happy** to be outside and away from the internet.
9. Today will be the best day!

❖ In Thailand, the Takhrai (lemongrass) is not only a culinary staple but also revered for its potent medicinal properties, traditionally used to alleviate fever and digestive issues.

1. วันนี้เรามี **สามสิบเอ็ด** ต้นไม้ในสวน.
2. แล้วดอกไม้ล่ะ?
3. มี **สามสิบสอง** ดอก.
4. หญ้านับไม่ได้เลย, แต่ใบไม้มี **สามสิบสาม** ใบ.
5. เย็นนี้ดูโทรทัศน์กันไหม?
6. ดี, มีข่าวอะไรบ้างในช่อง **สามสิบสี่**?
7. ไม่แน่ใจ, ใช้รีโมทหาดูสิ. รีโมทอยู่ทางซ้ายหรือขวา?
8. อยู่ทางขวา. แต่ฉันรู้สึกวิตกกังวลเรื่องข่าว.
9. ไม่ต้องกลัว, เราจะดู **สามสิบห้า** ช่อง, มีหนังสนุกๆ ดู.

✤ In Thai, when saying numbers 31-39, you contract "สามสิบ" (thirty) to "สามสิบเอ็ด" for 31, but for 32-39, you say them normally like "สามสิบสอง" for 32.

1. Wan nî rao mī **sām sìp 'ēt** tôn māi nai sūan.

2. Læo døk māi læ?

3. Mī **sām sìp sǫng** døk.

4. Yā náp māi dāi lēi, tæ̀ bai māi mī **sām sìp sǎm** bai.

5. Yēn nî dū torat'at'han kan māi?

6. Dī, mī khāo 'arai bāng nai chǫng **sām sìp sì**?

7. Māi næ̀ chuai, chái rīmot hā dū sī. Rīmot yû thāng sái rǔe khwā?

8. Yû thāng khwā. Tæ̀ chǎn rû sūk witok kangwon rûang khāo.

9. Māi tǫng klūa, rao cā dū **sām sìp h̄ā** chǫng, mī nāng sanūk sanūk dū.

1. Today we have **thirty-one** trees in the garden.
2. What about the flowers?
3. There are **thirty-two** flowers.
4. The grass is countless, but there are **thirty-three** leaves.
5. Shall we watch TV this evening?
6. Sure, what's on channel **thirty-four**?
7. Not sure, use the remote to find out. Is the remote on the left or right?
8. It's on the right. But I'm feeling anxious about the news.
9. Don't worry, we'll watch channel **thirty-five**, there are fun movies to watch.

✤ In Thai architecture, the number 9 is considered highly auspicious, influencing the design of royal buildings to often incorporate it, reflecting the belief in its power and the reverence for the king, who is traditionally associated with this number.

วันที่ 54: ดนตรีและความบันเทิง

1. คืนนี้เธออยากไปดู**คอนเสิร์ต**หรือไปดู**ภาพยนตร์**ที่โรง
ละคร?

2. ฉันอยากไปดู**คอนเสิร์ต**มากกว่า เพราะฉันชอบฟัง**เพลง**และ
ชอบดู**นักร้อง**กับวง**ดนตรี**เล่น.

3. ใช่ ฉันก็ชอบ**เพลง**จาก**วิทยุ**แต่การได้เห็นการ**เล่นสด**ๆ ที่
คอนเสิร์ตน่าตื่นเต้นกว่าเยอะ.

4. แล้วเธอชอบ**การเต้น**ไหม? บางทีใน**คอนเสิร์ต**อาจมีการ
แสดง**การเต้น**ที่สนุกสนาน.

5. ชอบสิ! การดู**การเต้น**ทำให้ฉันรู้สึกมีพลังและอยาก
เต้นตาม.

✤ In Thai, to talk about a specific movie or song, use the determiner "นั้น" (nán) after the noun, like "เพลงนั้น" (the song) or "หนังนั้น" (the movie).

1. Khūmnî̂ thêx yāk pai dū **khxnsērt** rēu pai dū **phāphyntr** thī **rōng lākhr**?

2. Chạn yāk pai dū **khxnsērt** mākkwā phrā chạn chxb fang **phleng** læa chxb dū **nakr̂xng** kạb wong **dontrī** len.

3. Chî chạn k̄hx chxb **phleng** cāk **withyū** tæ̀ kār dāi hĕn kān **len** s̄d s̄d thī **khxnsērt** nā theūn tĕn kwà yè.

4. Læa thêx chxb **kān tên** h̄ịm? Bāng thī nı **khxnsērt** xā mī kān s̄dæng **kān tên** thī s̄nunsnān.

5. Chxb s̄i! Kān dū **kān tên** thả k̄hị chạn rûs̄ūk mī phalāng læa yāk ten tām.

1. Do you want to go to a **concert** or see a **movie** at the **theater** tonight?
2. I'd rather go to a **concert** because I enjoy listening to **music** and watching **singers** and **bands** perform.
3. Yes, I also like **music** from the **radio** but seeing a live performance at a **concert** is much more exciting.
4. Do you like **dancing**? Sometimes at **concerts**, there might be fun **dance** performances.
5. Of course! Watching **dancing** makes me feel energized and makes me want to dance along.

♣ In Thailand, the haunting sound of the "khim," a traditional hammered dulcimer, is believed to connect the spiritual and earthly realms.

วันที่ 55: การเดินทางและการขนส่ง ภาค 3 ✒

1. ไปสนามบินยังไงดี?
2. นั่งรถไฟไปสถานีรถไฟแล้วต่อแท็กซี่.
3. ถ้าไปท่าเรือล่ะ?
4. ก็ได้, นั่งรถบัสไปท่าเรือเลย.
5. รถยนต์สะดวกกว่าไหม?
6. สะดวกแหละ แต่จะติดจราจรบนถนน.
7. แล้วเรือล่ะ?
8. เรือดีถ้าไปเกาะ.

✤ In Thai, to express quantity before a noun, use a quantifier like "สอง" (two) followed by a classifier appropriate to the noun, such as "คัน" for vehicles.

1. pāi **sānām bin** yang ngai dī?
2. nâng **rōt fai** pāi **sāthānī rōt fai** lǽo tô **thæksī**.
3. thā pāi **thā rēu** lā?
4. kô dāi, nâng **rōt bat** pāi **thā rēu** loei.
5. **rōt yon** sādwǎk kwā hai mai?
6. sādwǎk lǽo tæ̀ cà tīt **carǎchon** bon thānon.
7. lǽo **rēu** la?
8. **rēu** dī thā pāi kaw.

1. How should I get to the **airport**?
2. Take the **train** to the **train station** and then a **taxi**.
3. What if I'm going to the **pier**?
4. That works, take a **bus** straight to the **pier**.
5. Is taking a **car** more convenient?
6. It's convenient, but there will be **traffic** on the roads.
7. What about a **boat**?
8. A **boat** is good if you're going to an island.

✤ In Thailand, the legendary Queen Suriyothai rode into battle on an elephant to protect her kingdom, becoming a pioneering heroine in Thai history.

วันที่ 56: ช้อปปิ้ง ครั้งที่สอง

1. วันนี้เราจะไป**ศูนย์การค้า**กันไหม?
2. อยากไป**ซูเปอร์มาร์เก็ตหรือร้านขายของชำ**?
3. ฉันอยากซื้อเสื้อผ้าและเสื้อแจ็คเก็ต.
4. **ดูเครื่องประดับด้วยไหม**? อย่าง**สร้อยคอหรือต่างหู**.
5. ใช่, ฉันหวังว่าจะมี**ลดราคา**.
6. ถ้าเราซื้อหลายอย่าง เราอาจได้**ส่วนลดเพิ่ม**.
7. นั่นดีมาก! เราไปกันเลย.

✤ In Thai, to show possession, add "ของ" (khǒng) before the possessor, like "กระเป๋าของ เธอ" means "her bag."

1. Wannî rao cà pāi **sūnyā kān khā** kan mị̌?

2. Yàk pāi **sû pheṛ māř ket** rū **r̂ān khāy khǒng cham**?

3. Chạn xàk sū̌ **s̄eū̌x phā** læa **s̄eū̌x jǣk ket**.

4. Dū **kherū̌xng pradạb** dūay mị̌? Yàngx **s̄r̂xy khor** rū **t̀ầng hū**.

5. Chî, chạn h̄wạng wā ca mī **lōt rākhā**.

6. T̂hā rao sū̌ h̄lāy xyāng rao xāc dāi **s̄̀ùan lōt** phīm.

7. Nạn dī māk! Rao pāi kan loie.

1. Are we going to the **shopping center** today?
2. Do you want to go to the **supermarket** or the **grocery store**?
3. I want to buy some **clothes** and a **jacket**.
4. Should we also look at **jewelry**? Like **necklaces** or **earrings**.
5. Yes, I hope there are **sales**.
6. If we buy a lot, we might get an additional **discount**.
7. That's great! Let's go.

✤ In Thailand, the Chatuchak Weekend Market, one of the world's largest flea markets, spans over 35 acres and hosts more than 15,000 booths selling items from every corner of the country.

วันที่ 57: ร่างกายและสุขภาพ 2 🖋

1. เมื่อวานนี้ฉันไปศูนย์การค้า แล้วเจ็บ**หลัง**จากหิ้วของหนักๆ
2. จริงเหรอ? ฉันก็เจ็บ**แขน**เพราะยกของเยอะเหมือนกัน
3. แล้วเธอทำอย่างไรบ้าง?
4. ฉันพักและนวดเท้า ช่วยได้เยอะเลย
5. ฉันควรจะลองดูบ้าง แต่ฉันยังเจ็บ**หัว**จากเสียงดังใน คอนเสิร์ตเมื่อคืน
6. อ๋อ ฉันเข้าใจ คอนเสิร์ตวงดนตรีนั้นดังมาก
7. ใช่ แล้วฉันยังไม่ได้กินอะไรเลย อยากกิน**เนื้อสัตว์**กับ**ผัก**
8. ดีจัง ฉันก็หิวแล้ว ไปซูเปอร์มาร์เก็ตกันไหม?
9. ไปสิ!

✤ In Thai, to say "this" or "that" when talking about body parts or health, use "นี่" (nîi) for things close to you and "นั่น" (nán) for things far from you.

1. Mūa wăn nî chạn pai sūny kār khā læa cĕb **hlạng** càk hîw k̄hxng nạk nạk
2. Cìngrĕ r? Chạn k̄h cĕb **k̄hæn** pheụ̄x yk k̄hxng yeụ̄x mæ̃en kan
3. Læa thœ̄ thả xỳāng rị bāng?
4. Chạn phạk læa nwạd **thêā** chûay dị̂ yèo leīy
5. Chạn khụ̄an cā lxxng dū bāng tæ̀ chạn yang cĕb **hụ̄a** càk s̄īang dạng nı k̄hns̄ìrt mūa khn
6. X̀x chạn k̄hā chı̄ chı̄ k̄hns̄ìrt wong dontrī nạn dạng māk
7. Chı̀ læa chạn yang mị̀ dị̂ kın ʾārị læ̀ xyāk kın **nụ̄̂s̄ạtẁ** kạb **phạk**
8. Dī cạng chạn k̄h hūa læa pai sû phæ̀r̂ mārket kan h̄ịm?
9. Pai s̄ı!

164

1. Yesterday, I went to the mall and then hurt my **back** from carrying heavy stuff.
2. Really? I also hurt my **arm** from lifting a lot of things.
3. What did you do about it?
4. I rested and massaged my **feet**. It helped a lot.
5. I should try that, but I still have a **headache** from the loud noise at the concert last night.
6. Oh, I understand. That concert was really loud.
7. Yes, and I haven't eaten anything yet. I want to eat **meat** and **vegetables**.
8. That sounds great. I'm hungry too. Shall we go to the supermarket?
9. Let's go!

❧ In Thailand, it's common to use a blend of turmeric and lemongrass as a traditional remedy to alleviate muscle pain.

วันที่ 58: อาชีพและการทำงาน ตอนที่ 1

1. สวัสดีครับ คุณเป็น**หมอ**หรือ**ทันตแพทย์**ครับ?
2. ผมเป็น**ทันตแพทย์**ครับ และคุณล่ะ?
3. ผมเป็น**เชฟ**ครับ ชอบทำอาหาร เช่น ไก่พริกไทยดำเนย
4. น่าสนใจมากครับ ผมชอบกินอาหารที่มีชีส
5. คุณมีเพื่อนที่เป็น**นักเขียน**หรือ**นักแสดง**ไหมครับ?
6. มีครับ เพื่อนผมเป็น**นักเขียน** เขาชอบเดินทางโดยรถไฟ
7. ผมชอบเดินทางโดย**รถยนต์แดง**ครับ สะดวกดี
8. ผมก็ชอบครับ แต่บางครั้งก็นั่ง**รถบัส**ไปทำงาน
9. ดีจังครับ การเดินทางที่หลากหลายช่วยให้ชีวิตไม่น่า
   เบื่อนะครับ

✤ In Thai, to describe someone's profession, you use the structure "คน + [profession]" where "คน" means "person" and is used like "who is a" in English.

1. sawatdī khrap khun pen **mǫ** rū **thantaphæt** khrap?
2. phǫm pen **thantaphæt** khrap læa khun læ?
3. phǫm pen **chef** khrap chǫb tham āhān chěn kāi phrik thai dam nǫi
4. nā sanī mak khrap phǫm chǫb kin āhān thī mī chīs
5. khun mī phûan thī pen **nak khīan** rū **nak sǎdǎng** māi khrap?
6. mī khrap phûan phǫm pen **nak khīan** khǎo chǫb doēn thāng doī rotyon
7. phǫm chǫb doēn thāng doī **rotyon daēng** khrap sādūak dī
8. phǫm kǫ chǫb khrap tæ bāng khrang kǫ nāng **rot bas** pai tham ngān
9. dī jang khrap kān doēn thāng thī lāk lāi chūay hai chīwit māi nā bǫ nā khrap

1. Hello, are you a **doctor** or a **dentist**?
2. I am a **dentist**. And you?
3. I am a **chef**. I like cooking dishes like black pepper butter chicken.
4. That's very interesting. I like eating food with cheese.
5. Do you have a friend who is a **writer** or an **actor**?
6. Yes, my friend is a **writer**. He likes traveling by train.
7. I like traveling by **red car**. It's convenient.
8. I like it too, but sometimes I take the **bus** to work.
9. That's great. Having various ways to travel makes life more interesting.

✤ In Thailand, the intricate art of fruit carving began in the 14th century, originally crafted to decorate the royal tables.

วันที่ 59: อุปกรณ์ในบ้าน ชุดที่ 2 ✎

1. ดู **โซฟา** ใหม่ของฉันสิ
2. สวยมาก! แล้วนี่ **เตาอบ** ใหม่ด้วยหรือเปล่า?
3. ใช่, ฉันซื้อมาพร้อมกับ **ตู้เย็น** ใหม่ด้วย
4. โอ้, แล้ว **โคมไฟ** นั่นล่ะ?
5. ฉันได้มาจากร้านขายของชำ และนี่ **โต๊ะ** กับ **เก้าอี้** ใหม่
6. ห้องนอนมี **เตียง** ใหม่ไหม?
7. มีสิ, และฉันยังเปลี่ยน **หน้าต่าง** และ **ประตู** ใหม่ด้วย
8. ว้าว, บ้านของเธอดูดีมากเลย
9. ขอบคุณมาก! ฉันยังคิดจะซื้อ **นาฬิกา** ใหม่อีกด้วย

✤ In Thai, to talk about indefinite household items, you can use "บาง" (some) before the noun, like "บางเก้าอี้" for "some chairs".

1. duu **sōfā** mài khǎwng chǎn sǐ
2. sǔai mâak! láew nîi **tao op** mài dûai rěu bplào?
3. châi, chǎn súe mâa phrôm kap **tûi yen** mài dûai
4. ôh, láew **khōm lāi** nân là?
5. chǎn dâi maa jàak ráan khǎi khǎwng cham láew nîi **tó** kap **kâo îi** mài
6. hông nâwn mii **tīang** mài mǎi?
7. mii sǐ, láew chǎn yang bpliian **nâa tàang** láew **pratû** mài dûai
8. wáaw, bâan khǎwng thêo duu dii mâak ləəi
9. khâwp khun mâak! chǎn yang khít jà súe **nālikā** mài ìik dûai

1. Check out my new **sofa**.
2. It's so beautiful! And is that a new **oven** too?
3. Yes, I bought it along with a new **refrigerator**.
4. Oh, and what about that **lamp** over there?
5. I got it from a convenience store, and here's a new **table** and **chairs**.
6. Is there a new **bed** in the bedroom?
7. Yes, and I also replaced the **windows** and **doors**.
8. Wow, your house looks amazing.
9. Thank you so much! I'm also thinking of buying a new **clock**.

✤ Thailand invented the energy-saving "Tubular Skylight," illuminating homes with natural light without electricity.

วันที่ ๖๐: การวัดและขนาด 🌱

1. **ขนาด**ของโต๊ะหลังนี้เท่าไหร่คะ?
2. **ความยาว**ประมาณ 150 **เซนติเมตร, ความกว้าง** 75 **เซนติเมตร และ ความสูง** 90 **เซนติเมตร** ครับ.
3. แล้ว**น้ำหนัก**ล่ะคะ?
4. ประมาณ 20 **กิโลกรัม** ครับ.
5. โอเคค่ะ, ตู้เย็น**ขนาด**เท่าไหร่บ้าง?
6. **ความสูง** 180 **เซนติเมตร, ความกว้าง** 70 **เซนติเมตร** ครับ.
7. มี**รูปร่าง**สวยไหมคะ?
8. ใช่ครับ, มันมี**รูปร่าง**ทันสมัยและสวยงามมากครับ.
9. ขอบคุณค่ะ, ฉันจะพิจารณาซื้อ.

✤ In Thai, to describe the size or measurement of something happening now, we use the present participle by adding "กำลัง" before the verb, like "กำลังวัด" for "measuring."

1. **khanāt** khǭng tô h̄lang nî thâo h̄ịr̀ị kha?
2. **khwām yāo** pramān 150 **sen timet, khwām kwāng** 75 **sen timet læ khwām s̄ūng** 90 **sen timet** khrạb.
3. læw **n̂ảh̄nạk** læ kha?
4. pramān 20 **kilo kram** khrạb.
5. o khe kha, tû yen **khanāt** thâo h̄ịr̀ị bāng?
6. **khwām s̄ūng** 180 **sen timet, khwām kwāng** 70 **sen timet** khrạb.
7. mī **rūp rāng** s̄wy m̀ị kha?
8. ch̀ị khrạb, man mī **rūp rāng** than samay læ s̄wy ngām māk khrạb.
9. khxbkhun kha, chạn c̄hā phicārn̒ s̄ū.

DAY 60: MEASUREMENTS AND SIZE

1. **Size** of this table, please?
2. **Length** is about 150 **centimeters, width 75 centimeters, and height** 90 **centimeters**.
3. What about the **weight**?
4. It's about 20 **kilograms**.
5. Okay, how about the **size** of the refrigerator?
6. **Height** 180 **centimeters, width** 70 **centimeters**.
7. Does it have a nice **shape**?
8. Yes, it has a very modern and beautiful **shape**.
9. Thank you, I'll consider buying it.

✤ In ancient Thailand, the length of one's forearm was used as a standard measurement unit called a "sok."

CHALLENGE NO. 6

RECORD A SHORT AUDIO WHERE YOU TALK ABOUT YOUR PROGRESS IN THAI.

การเคารพความแตกต่างเป็นกุญแจสู่ความเข้าใจ

Respecting differences is the key to understanding.

วันที่ 61: อาหารและโภชนาการ 2 ✿

1. วันนี้เราจะกินอะไรดี?
2. ฉันอยากกิน**พาสต้า**กับ**เนื้อวัวและชีส**.
3. ดีมาก! ฉันจะใส่**เนยและพริกไทย**ด้วยนะ.
4. แล้วของหวานล่ะ? มีอะไรบ้าง?
5. **มีไอศกรีม**. อยากกินไหม?
6. อยากสิ! แต่ฉันอยากกิน**ข้าวกับหมู**ด้วยได้ไหม?
7. ได้สิ. ฉันจะทำให้.
8. แล้ว**ขนมปัง**ล่ะ? มีไหม?
9. มี, ฉันจะทำ**ขนมปังกับไก่**ให้.

✤ In Thai, to form the past participle of a verb related to food, like "cooked" or "eaten," add "แล้ว" (láew) after the verb.

1. Wan nī rao cà kīn à rai dī?
2. Chạn xỳàk kīn **phās tā** kap **nửa wua læ chī s**.
3. Dī māk! Chạn cà sài **neī** læ **phrīk thai** dūai ná.
4. Lǽo k̄hngx wān lạ? Mī à rai bāng?
5. Mī **ī sà krīm**. Xỳàk kīn mị?
6. Xỳàk sì! Tæ chạn xỳàk kīn **k̄hāw** kap **mū** dūai dị mị?
7. Dị sì. Chạn cà tham h̄ị.
8. Lǽo **k̄hnǁm pāng** lạ? Mī mị?
9. Mī, chạn cà tham **k̄hnǁm pāng** kap **kài** h̄ị.

DAY 61: FOOD AND NUTRITION II

1. What should we eat today?
2. I want to eat **pasta** with **beef** and **cheese**.
3. Great! I'll add **butter** and **black pepper** too.
4. What about dessert? What do we have?
5. We have **ice cream**. Do you want some?
6. Yes, please! But can I also have **rice** with **pork**?
7. Of course. I'll make it for you.
8. And what about **bread**? Do we have any?
9. Yes, I'll make **bread** with **chicken** for you.

✤ In Thailand, the beloved dish Pad Thai was actually popularized in the 1930s as part of a campaign to modernize and economize food consumption while promoting Thai nationalism.

วันที่ ๖๒: วันในสัปดาห์ ✏️

1. **วันจันทร์** นี้เราจะไปโรงพยาบาลไหม?

2. ไม่, **วันพุธ** เราจะไป.

3. **วันอังคาร** นี้เราจะทำอะไร?

4. เราจะทำพาสต้าที่บ้าน. ฉันจะใช้เตาอบ.

5. แล้ว **วันพฤหัสบดี** ล่ะ?

6. เราจะไปซื้อต้นไม้และดอกไม้.

7. **วันศุกร์** เราจะพักผ่อนที่บ้าน.

8. ดีจัง! **วันเสาร์** และ **วันอาทิตย์** เราจะทำอะไร?

9. **สุดสัปดาห์** เราจะไปเดินเล่นในสวน, ดูต้นไม้และหญ้า.

✤ In Thai, to talk about activities done on specific days, we use the day of the week followed by the activity in gerund form, like "วันเสาร์กินข้าว" (On Saturday, eating rice).

1. **Wan jan** nī rao cà pài rōng phayābān mǎi?

2. Mai, **wan phut** rao cà pài.

3. **Wan angkhān** nī rao cà tham arai?

4. Rao cà tham phǎ štā thî bān. Chǎn cà chái tāo op.

5. Lǽo **wan phrūhatsadī** lǽ?

6. Rao cà pài šūe ton māi lǽa dǫk māi.

7. **Wan šukhř** rao cà phakphǒn thî bān.

8. Dī cang! **Wan šǎř** lǽa **wan āthit** rao cà tham arai?

9. **Sutsapdǎň** rao cà pài doēn len nai šūan, du ton māi lǽa yā.

1. Are we going to the hospital this **Monday**?
2. No, we will go on **Wednesday**.
3. What about this **Tuesday**?
4. We will make pasta at home. I'll use the oven.
5. And **Thursday**?
6. We will go buy some plants and flowers.
7. **Friday** we will rest at home.
8. Great! What about **Saturday** and **Sunday**?
9. **Over the weekend**, we will go for a walk in the park, look at the trees and grass.

✤ In Thailand, each day of the week is associated with a specific color and celestial body, influencing people's clothing choices for good luck.

วันที่ 63 : เวลาและฤดูกาล

1. วันนี้ร้อนมาก
2. ใช่, แต่พรุ่งนี้จะหนาวหรือไม่?
3. ไม่แน่นอน, แต่เช้านี้หนาวนิดหน่อย
4. เย็นนี้จะออกไปไหนไหม?
5. อาจจะไปเดินเล่น ถ้าไม่ร้อนเกินไป
6. คืนนี้เย็นกว่าวันนี้หรือไม่?
7. คิดว่าน่าจะเย็นกว่านะ เพราะเข้าสู่ฤดูใบไม้ผลิ
8. ดีจัง, ฉันชอบอากาศเย็นๆ
9. ใช่, เย็นและสบายดี

✤ In Thai, to express the infinitive form of a verb related to weather or seasons, you often use the word "ทำ" (to do/make) before the weather verb, like "ทำให้ร้อน" (to make hot).

1. **wan nî** rɔ́n māk
2. châi, tæ̀ **phrûng nî** cǎ **nǎo** rɐ̌u mâi?
3. mâi nɛ̂nɔ̌n, tæ̀ **cháo** nî **nǎo** nít nɔ̀i
4. **yen** nî cǎ ɔ̀k pai nǎi mǎi?
5. àt cǎ pai dɔ̄ēn len tʰâ mâi **rɔ́n** gɔ̄ēn pai
6. **khuen** nî **yen** gwà **wan nî** rɐ̌u mâi?
7. khít wâ nâcǎ **yen** gwà ná pʰrɔ́ cǎo sù **rûdu phlǐ**
8. dī cang, cʰǎn chɔ̌b àkāt **yen** ɲ
9. châi, **yen** læ sàbāi dī

1. **Today** is very hot.
2. Yes, but will **tomorrow** be **cold**?
3. Not sure, but this **morning** was a bit **cold**.
4. Are you going out this **evening**?
5. Might go for a walk if it's not too **hot**.
6. Will **tonight** be **cooler** than **today**?
7. I think it will be **cooler**, as we're entering **spring**.
8. That's great, I like **cool** weather.
9. Yes, **cool** and comfortable.

✤ In Thailand, the song "เพลงของฤดู" (Songs of the Seasons) beautifully encapsulates the country's love for its tropical seasons, celebrating the lush monsoon and the vibrant summer through its lyrics.

วันที่ 64: ครอบครัว ภาค 2

1. **หลานชาย** วันนี้ ป้า ทำอะไรครับ?
2. **ป้า** วันนี้ป้าทำสปาเก็ตตี้ เนย และเนื้อวัวค่ะ.
3. **หลานสาว** พรุ่งนี้มีคอนเสิร์ต นักร้องที่เราชอบนะคะ.
4. **ลุง** วันพฤหัสบดีนี้ **ลูกพี่ลูกน้อง** กับ **คู่หมั้น** จะไปดู ภาพยนตร์.
5. **หลานชาย** วันศุกร์ **เพื่อนร่วมงาน** จะมาบ้านเรา.
6. **หลานสาว** แล้ววันอังคารล่ะคะ?
7. **ลุง** วันอังคาร **น้า** จะทำพริกไทยไก่ครับ.

✤ In Thai, adding "**พ่อ**" (father) or "**แม่**" (mother) before a family member's title makes it paternal or maternal, respectively.

1. **Lān chāi** Wan nī **pā** tham arai khrap?
2. **Pā** Wan nī pā tham sapākettī, noei, læa nūa wua khà.
3. **Lān sāo** Phrung nī mī khānsœ̄t, nakhrǭng thī rao chǭp ná khà.
4. **Lung** Wan phruehasabodī nī **lūk phī lūk nong** kap **khū̂ ȟmạn** cà pai du phāphyantr.
5. **Lān chāi** Wan ŝuk **phûan rūamngān** cà mā bān rao.
6. **Lān sāo** Læa wan angkhān là khà?
7. **Lung** Wan angkhān **ná** cà tham phrik thai kài khrap.

1. **Nephew:** What are you doing today, **Aunt**?
2. **Aunt:** Today, I'm making spaghetti with butter and beef.
3. **Niece:** There's a concert tomorrow by the singer we like.
4. **Uncle:** This Thursday, **cousins** and **fiancés** are going to the movies.
5. **Nephew:** On Friday, **co-workers** will come to our house.
6. **Niece:** What about Tuesday?
7. **Uncle:** On Tuesday, **Uncle** will make pepper chicken.

✤ In Thailand, it's common for families to share tales of household spirits, believed to protect the home and bring good fortune.

วันที่ 65: ทิศทางและสถานที่ III

1. **ตรงไป** ที่สนามบิน หรือ เลี้ยว **ซ้าย** ไปรถไฟ?
2. ขวา ค่ะ, รถบัส **ใกล้** กว่า.
3. รถยนต์จอด **บน** หรือ **ล่าง**?
4. **ล่าง** ครับ, **ใกล้** ห้องน้ำ.
5. **หยุด** ที่โซฟา หรือ **ตรงไป** เตียง?
6. **ตรงไป** ค่ะ, เตียง **ไกล** จากโซฟา.
7. เก้าอี้อยู่ **ระหว่าง** โต๊ะกับห้องน้ำ?
8. ใช่ครับ, **ใกล้** โต๊ะมากกว่า.

✤ In Thai, to indicate direction towards something, add "ไป" (pai) after the place or direction word.

1. **troṅ pai** thī̀ šnāmbin h̄rụ̄x **lîyw šāi** pai rthfai?
2. khwā kh̀ā, rthbạs **k̄hlāi** kwas̄.
3. rthynt̒ cxd **bn** h̄rụ̄x **l̀āng**?
4. **l̀āng** khrạb, **k̄hlāi** h̄̀xngn̂å.
5. **hyud** thī̀ sofā h̄rụ̄x **troṅ pai** tīyng?
6. **troṅ pai** kh̀ā, tīyng **kิlāi** cāk sofā.
7. kêāxî̂ xyū̀ **raḥ̄wāng** tôā kạb h̄̀xngn̂å?
8. chì khrạb, **k̄hlāi** tôā mākkwas̄.

1. **Straight ahead** to the airport, or **turn left** to the train?
2. **Right**, please, the bus is **closer**.
3. Is the car parked **on top** or **below**?
4. **Below, sir, close** to the bathroom.
5. **Stop** at the sofa, or **go straight** to the bed?
6. **Go straight**, please, the bed is **far** from the sofa.
7. Is the chair **between** the table and the bathroom?
8. Yes, sir, **closer** to the table.

✤ In Thai literature, the epic journey of Phra Abhai Mani, written by Sunthorn Phu, show-cases a hero's adventures across magical lands and seas, embodying the rich tapestry of Thai folklore and imagination.

วันที่ 66: อารมณ์ ภาค 2 ✒️

1. วันนี้ฉัน**ตื่นเต้น**มาก ไปศูนย์การค้ากันไหม?
2. ฉัน**กระวนกระวาย**นิดหน่อย แต่ก็อยากไป.
3. ฉัน**กังวล**ว่าจะมีคนเยอะไหมนะ.
4. ไม่ต้อง**วิตกกังวล**หรอก ฉันว่าน่าจะโอเค.
5. ฉันหวังว่าจะซื้อเสื้อแจ็คเก็ตได้ จะ**ภูมิใจ**มากๆ.
6. ถ้าไม่เจอล่ะ? จะ**โกรธ**ไหม?
7. ไม่หรอก ฉันจะพยายาม**ผ่อนคลาย**และไม่**เครียด**.
8. ดีมาก ฉันก็หวังว่าเราจะ**สุข**ใจกับการช้อปปิ้งวันนี้.
9. ใช่ แม้จะ**สับสน**บ้าง แต่ก็**ตื่นเต้น**.

✤ In Thai, to express emotions in the past or future, we use the verbs for 'to be' (เป็น, อยู่, จะ) before the emotion word, like "I was happy" becomes "ฉันเป็นสุข" (I was happy).

1. wannī chạn **từn tên** māk pai sūný kār k̄hā kạn h̄ịm?
2. chạn **krā wnn krā wāy** nithòxy tæ̀ k̂ xỳāk pai.
3. chạn **kạngwn** wâ ch̀ mī khn yè h̄ịm ná.
4. mị̀ t̂xng **wítk kạngwn** h̄r̀k chạn wâ nâcà k̄h xk.
5. chạn h̄wạng wâ cà sữx jæk kĕt d̂ị cà **phūmị jai** māk māk.
6. t̄ĥā mị̀ cer l̀ạ? cà **krîth** h̄ịm?
7. mị̀ h̄r̀k chạn cà phyāyām **ph̀xn klāy** læa mị̀ **khrīd**.
8. dī māk chạn k̂ h̄wạng wâ rao cà **sukjai** kạb kār chôppīng wannī.
9. cị̀ mæ̀ cà **sạb s̄n** b̀āng tæ̀ k̂ **từn tên**.

1. Today, I'm **excited** a lot. Want to go to the mall?
2. I'm a bit **nervous**, but I still want to go.
3. I'm **worried** about it being too crowded.
4. No need to **worry**; I think it'll be okay.
5. I hope to buy a jacket; I'll be **proud**.
6. What if we don't find one? Will you be **angry**?
7. Not at all, I'll try to **relax** and not **stress**.
8. Great, I also hope we'll **enjoy** our shopping today.
9. Yes, even though it's a bit **confusing**, I'm excited.

✤ In Thailand, traditional mask-making for the Khon dance involves crafting the masks to express fixed emotions, symbolizing the eternal nature of the characters' roles in the epic Ramakien.

วันที่ 67: เทคโนโลยีและสื่อ ✍

1. วันนี้เราใช้ **อินเทอร์เน็ต** ทำอะไรบ้าง?
2. ฉันใช้ **สมาร์ทโฟน** เล่น **โซเชียลเน็ตเวิร์ก** และดู **บล็อก** น่าสนใจ.
3. เธอเข้า **เว็บไซต์** ไหนดี?
4. ฉันชอบเข้า **เว็บไซต์** ที่มี **แอปพลิเคชัน** เรียนภาษา.
5. ใช้ **อีเมล** ติดต่องานบ่อยไหม?
6. ใช่, และฉันยังใช้ **ไวไฟ** เพื่อเชื่อมต่อ **ออนไลน์** ตลอดเวลา.
7. การเรียกดูด้วย **เบราว์เซอร์** สะดวกดีไหม?
8. สะดวกมาก, ฉันสามารถค้นหาข้อมูลได้ทุกที่ทุกเวลา.

✤ In Thai, to express the desire to do something related to technology and media, like "to watch" a movie or "to play" a video game, we often use the infinitive form of the verb, such as "ดู" for "to watch" or "เล่น" for "to play."

1. wan nî rao chái **in thêrxnet** tham àrai bâng?
2. chạn chái **smārt fōn** lên **so chīan net wêrk** læa du **blǫ̀k** nâ sǒn jai.
3. thǿ khao **web sai** nǎi dī?
4. chạn chǒp khao **web sai** thī mī **æp phlik chēn** rīan phās̄'ā.
5. chái **I mel** tìt ìxngān bxy mǎi?
6. chǎi, læa chạn yang chái **wai fai** phêūa chêūam ìx **x xn lain** tlxd welā.
7. kān rīak du dūay **bro ʂeūr** sà dūak dī mǎi?
8. sà dūak māk, chạn ʂāmārt khạn h̄ǎ khāmūl dâi thuk thî thuk welā.

1. What did we use the **internet** for today?
2. I used my **smartphone** to play on **social networks** and watch interesting **blogs**.
3. Which **websites** do you recommend?
4. I like visiting **websites** that have language learning **applications**.
5. Do you often use **email** for work communication?
6. Yes, and I also use **Wi-Fi** to stay **online** all the time.
7. Is browsing with a **browser** convenient?
8. Very convenient, I can search for information anywhere, anytime.

✤ In Thailand, the first newspaper was introduced in 1844 by an American missionary, marking the beginning of the country's press evolution.

วันที่ 68: การอ่านและศิลปะ ✐

1. วันนี้เธออ่าน**หนังสือ**อะไรอยู่หรือเปล่า?
2. อ่าน**นวนิยาย**อยู่ครับ แล้วเธอล่ะ?
3. ฉันชอบ**กวีนิพนธ์**มาก แต่วันนี้ฉันกำลังฝึกวาด**รูป**อยู่.
4. น่าสนใจจัง! เธอชอบ**จิตรกรรม**หรือ**การถ่ายภาพ** มากกว่ากัน?
5. ฉันชอบ**การถ่ายภาพ**มากกว่า มันทำให้ฉันได้เก็บความ ทรงจำ.
6. ฉันเข้าใจ แต่ฉันชอบ**การร้องเพลง**มากกว่าทุกอย่าง.
7. นั่นก็ดีนะ การมีงานอดิเรกทำให้ชีวิตสนุกขึ้น.

✤ In Thai, to form the participle mode for actions related to reading and arts, add "กำลัง" before the verb to show the action is currently happening.

1. Wannî thởè xàn **nạngṣụ̄x** xarị̀ xỳ h̄rụ̄x pělā?
2. Xàn **nạwniyāy** xỳ khrạb læw thởè lạ?
3. Chạn chxb **kwiniphntĥ** māk tæ̀ wannî chạn kảmlạng fụk **wād rūp** xỳ.
4. Ǹā s̄nịj cạng! Thởè chxb **citrkrrm** h̄rụ̄x **kār th̀āy phāph** mākkwà kạn?
5. Chạn chxb **kār th̀āy phāph** mākkwà man thạng h̄ị̂ chạn dị̂ kæb khwām s̄ngcảm.
6. Chạn k̄hêā cı dæ̀ chạn chxb **kār r̂xng pheīng** mākkwà thukxỳng.
7. Nạn k̄h̀ dī ṇa kār mī ngān xdi rek thạng h̄ị̂ chīwit s̄nuk khȅụ̄n.

1. Are you reading a **book** today by any chance?
2. I'm reading a **novel**. How about you?
3. I really like **poetry**, but today I'm practicing **drawing**.
4. That's interesting! Do you prefer **painting** or **photography**?
5. I prefer **photography** more. It allows me to capture memories.
6. I understand, but I like **singing** more than anything.
7. That's nice. Having hobbies makes life more enjoyable.

✦ In Thailand, the Bangkok National Museum, once a palace, houses the largest collection of Thai art and artifacts in the country.

วันที่ 69: การเดินทางและสถานที่ II 🌱

1. ฉันจะไปสนามบิน ควรเรียก**แท็กซี่**หรือไปสถานีรถไฟดี?
2. ถ้าเร่งด่วน แนะนำให้เรียก**แท็กซี่**เลย แต่ถ้ามีเวลา ไปสถานี **รถไฟ**ก็ดี
3. ถึงที่พักแล้ว ฉันจะพักที่**โรงแรม**หรือ**ที่พักแบบหอพัก**ดี?
4. ถ้าอยากสะดวกสบาย แนะนำ**โรงแรม** แต่ถ้าอยากประหยัด ลอง**ที่พักแบบหอพัก**
5. ฉันกังวลเรื่อง**กระเป๋าเดินทาง** มันจะหนักเกินไปไหม?
6. ถ้าเดินทางไกล พยายามใช้**กระเป๋าเป้**จะดีกว่า เพราะ สะดวกกว่า
7. ขอบคุณนะ ฉันจะจำไว้

✤ In Thai, to express the action of doing something as a gerund, like "traveling," add "การ" before the verb, turning it into "การเดินทาง."

1. Chạn c̀ā pị **s̄nāmbin** khwr rīykh **thæks̄ī** h̄rụ̄x pị **s̄thānī rthfị** dī?

2. Thả r̀xng d̀wn nænạm h̄î c̀ā rīykh **thæks̄ī** lxy tæ̀ thả mī welā pị **s̄thānī rthfị** k̆dī

3. Thụng thī phạk læw chạn c̀ā phạk thī **rōngræm** h̄rụ̄x **thī phạk bæb h̄xphạk** dī?

4. Thả xỳāng s̄ādws̄bāy nænạm **rōngræm** tæ̀ thả xỳāng prahyạd lxxng **thī phạk bæb h̄xphạk**

5. Chạn kạngwl rêụ̀xng **krạp̆ĕā den thāng** man c̄ā h̄nạk kīn tı mị̀?

6. Thả den thāng kịl phạyāyām chî **krạp̆ĕā pê** c̄ā dī kwdā phr̂x s̄ādwkwdā

7. K̄hxbkhuṇ nạ chạn c̄ā cam wị̂

1. Should I call a **taxi** or go to the **train station** to get to the **airport**?
2. If you're in a hurry, I recommend calling a **taxi** right away, but if you have time, going to the **train station** is also good.
3. Now that I've arrived, should I stay at a **hotel** or a **hostel**?
4. If you want comfort, I recommend a **hotel**, but if you want to save money, try a **hostel**.
5. I'm worried about my **luggage**. Will it be too heavy?
6. If you're traveling far, it's better to use a **backpack** because it's more convenient.
7. Thank you, I'll remember that.

✤ In Thailand, the Erawan Shrine in Bangkok, originally created to appease mischievous spirits during the construction of a luxury hotel, is now a bustling spiritual site where thousands come to seek blessings.

วันที่ 70: ตัวเลข 11-20 🌾

1. วันนี้ฉันจะไปสนามบิน เวลา **สิบเอ็ด** โมงเช้า
2. ฉันจะไปสถานีรถไฟ เวลา **สิบสอง** โมงครึ่ง
3. คุณจะใช้**แท็กซี่**ไปหรือเปล่า?
4. ไม่, ฉันจะจอง**โรงแรม**ผ่านเว็บไซต์ แล้วเดินทางไปด้วยสมาร์ทโฟนของฉัน
5. ฉันเห็นอากาศวันนี้ชื้นมาก ต้องระวัง**เสียงฟ้าร้อง**
6. ใช่, ฉันเช็ค**พยากรณ์อากาศ**บนแอปพลิเคชันแล้ว บอกว่าจะมีฟ้าผ่าเวลาสิบห้าโมง
7. ดีจัง, ฉันจะออนไลน์หา**ที่พักที่มีอินเทอร์เน็ตดีๆ** รอบๆ **ยี่สิบ** โมง
8. ฉันหวังว่าคุณจะหาเจอนะ
9. ขอบคุณมาก!

✤ In Thai, to form numbers 11-19, add the word "sip" (meaning ten) before the numbers 1-9, but for 20, use "yee sip" instead, showing a change in aspect from simple counting to a new tens place.

1. Wannî chạn cà pāi **s̄nāmbin** welā **s̄ibxd** mong cheā
2. Chạn cà pāi **s̄thānī rthfị** welā **s̄bs̄xng** mong khreụ̄ng
3. Khun cà chî **thæks̄ī̂** pāi h̄rụ̄x bplào?
4. Mị̀, chạn cà cxng **rongræm** phạn **webs̄ị̂t** læw dein thāng pāi d̂uay **s̄mārt̒fon** k̄hxng chạn
5. Chạn h̄en **ākās̄** wannî **chụ̂n** māk t̂xng rawạng **s̄īyng f̂ā r̂xng**
6. Chî, chạn chek **phayākorn̒ ākās̄** bn æpphlikhechạn læw b̀x wâ chà mī **f̂ā ph̀ā** welā **s̄b̀xh̄̂ā** mong
7. Dī cạng, chạn cà xnlịn h̄ā **thī phạk** thī mī **inthexr̒net̒** dī dī rxb rxb **yīs̄ib** mong
8. Chạn h̄wạng wâ khun cà h̄ā ceụ̂x ná
9. K̄hxbkhum māk!

192

1. Today, I'm going to the **airport** at **eleven** in the morning.
2. I will go to the **train station** at **twelve-thirty**.
3. Are you going to take a **taxi**?
4. No, I will book a **hotel** through a **website** and then travel there with my **smartphone**.
5. I see the **weather** today is very **humid**. Be careful of **thunder**.
6. Yes, I checked the **weather forecast** on the **application** and it says there will be **lightning** at **fifteen** o'clock.
7. Great, I will go online to look for **accommodations** with good **internet** around **twenty** o'clock.
8. I hope you find one.
9. Thank you very much!

✤ In Thai art, numbers often symbolize traditional beliefs, where the number 9, representing prosperity and power, is especially auspicious due to its pronunciation being similar to the word for "progress" in Thai.

CHALLENGE NO. 7

ENGAGE IN A 15-MINUTE CONVERSATION
IN THAI ON EVERYDAY TOPICS.

ความอดทนเป็นหัวใจของการเรียนรู้

Patience is the heart of learning.

วันที่ 71: ตัวเลข 21 ถึง 30

1. เธอมีหนังสือ **ยี่สิบเอ็ด** เล่มไหม?
2. ไม่, ฉันมี **ยี่สิบสอง** เล่ม.
3. ในนั้นมีนวนิยายกี่เล่ม?
4. **ยี่สิบ** เล่มเป็นนวนิยาย.
5. แล้วกวีนิพนธ์ล่ะ?
6. มี **สอง** เล่ม.
7. น่าสนใจจัง! คุณชอบอ่านเรื่องอะไรมากที่สุด?
8. ฉันชอบนิยาย **มากที่สุด**.
9. ดีจัง! ฉันก็ชอบเหมือนกัน.

✤ In Thai, to form numbers from 21 to 29, you say "twenty" (ยี่สิบ yì sìp) followed by the digit, but for 30, you simply say "thirty" (สามสิบ sǎam sìp) without adding a digit.

1. Thœ mī nạngs<u>ร</u>ū **yìsibed** lem mị?
2. Mị, ōhạn mī **yìsibsฺxng** lem.
3. Nı nạn mī nwạnyāykī lem?
4. **Yìsib** lem pĕn nwạnyāy.
5. Læw kwnīphnth læ?
6. Mī **sฺxng** lem.
7. Ǹā sncı jạng! Khun chxb xān ru̇ng ῾rị māk thỉ sุud?
8. Ōhạn chxb nyāy **māk thỉ sุud**.
9. Dī cạng! Ōhạn k̄h ōhxb mǔn kạn.

1. Do you have **twenty-one** books?
2. No, I have **twenty-two**.
3. How many of those are novels?
4. **Twenty** of them are novels.
5. And what about poetry?
6. There are **two**.
7. Interesting! What do you like reading the most?
8. I like novels **the most**.
9. Great! I like them too.

✤ In Thailand, the number 9 is considered lucky because it sounds like the word for "progress" in Thai, often influencing mathematical choices in pricing and architecture.

วันที่ 72: หลากหลาย ตอนที่ 1

1. วันนี้เราจะไป**พิพิธภัณฑ์**ไหม?
2. อยากไปมาก! ฉันอ่านใน**ปฏิทิน**ว่ามีเทศกาลวัฒนธรรมชาว พื้นเมือง.
3. เราต้องดู**ตารางเวลา**รถไฟหรือแท็กซี่เพื่อไปที่นั่น.
4. ใช่, และฉันอยากเรียนรู้เกี่ยวกับ**ประวัติศาสตร์**และ **ประเพณี**ของพวกเขา.
5. หลังจากนั้นเราจะไปหาที่**สบายๆ**กินข้าวกัน.
6. ดีมาก! ฉันหวังว่าจะเจอ**นักท่องเที่ยว**คนอื่นๆ ที่สนใจ **วัฒนธรรม**เหมือนกัน.
7. แน่นอน, มันจะเป็นวันที่ดี.

✤ In Thai, verbs can change their meaning slightly by adding or removing particles, affecting how many objects they can have.

1. Wan nī rao cā pai **phiphithaphanthū** mai?

2. Yāk pai māk! Chaṇ ān nai **patithin** wā mī **thētsakān** watthanatham chāo phūenmueang.

3. Rao tǒng dū **tārāngwelā** rothfai rēu thaeksī pheūa pai thī nan.

4. Chai, læa chaṇ yāk rīanrū keīywkāp **prawattisāt** læa **praphēnī** khǒng phūak khǒ.

5. Lǎngcaṇ rao cā pai hā thī **sabāiyāi** kin khāo kan.

6. Dī māk! Chaṇ wang wā cā cē **nakthǒngthīāw** khon 'ūn'ūn thī sončhai **watthanatham** mūran kan.

7. Ǣnǣn, man cā pen wan thī dī.

1. Are we going to the **museum** today?
2. I really want to! I read in the **calendar** that there's a **festival** of indigenous culture.
3. We need to check the **train schedule** or taxi to get there.
4. Yes, and I want to learn about their **history** and **traditions**.
5. After that, we'll find a **cozy** place to eat.
6. Great! I hope to meet other **tourists** interested in **culture** as well.
7. Definitely, it's going to be a good day.

✤ In Thailand, there's a festival where people launch thousands of lanterns into the sky to ward off bad luck.

วันที่ 73: การทำอาหารและห้องครัว II ✎

1. วันนี้เราจะทำอะไรกินดี?
2. ลองทำ**จาน**ไก่ใน**เตาอบ**ไหม?
3. ดีมาก! เราต้องใช้**มีด**หั่นไก่ก่อนนะ.
4. ใช่, แล้วเราต้องใช้**กระทะ**ผัดผักด้วย.
5. อย่าลืม**หม้อ**ต้มซุปนะ.
6. ใช่, และเราต้องเตรียม**ส้อม**และ**ช้อน**ด้วย.
7. หลังจากนั้นเราจะเก็บอาหารที่เหลือใน**ตู้เย็น**.
8. ถ้าทำขนมปัง เราต้องใช้**เครื่องปิ้งขนมปัง**ด้วย.
9. ดีมาก, ทุกอย่างพร้อมแล้ว!

✤ In Thai, to make a verb transitive and show that someone is doing the action, add the word "ให้" (hâi) before the verb.

1. Wannî rao cà tham àrai kin dī?
2. L̀ong tham **cān** kài nai **tāo òp** mǎi?
3. Dī māk! Rao t̂xng chái **mīd** h̀an kài k̀xn ná.
4. Chài, læa rao t̂xng chái **krathǎ** phạd phạk dūay.
5. Yà lǔem **m̂ǒ** tôm sūp ná.
6. Chài, læa rao t̂xng triam **s̄̂xm** læa **chôn** dūay.
7. H̄lạngcāk nán rao cà kĕb āh̄ār thī̀ h̄lǒo nai **tû̂ yen**.
8. Thâ tham khanom pāng, rao t̂xng chái **kher̂xng pīng khanom pāng** dūay.
9. Dī māk, thuk xyāng phr̂ǒm læw!

1. What should we make to eat today?
2. How about trying a **chicken** dish in the **oven**?
3. Great idea! We need to use a **knife** to cut the chicken first.
4. Right, and we also need to use a **pan** to stir-fry the vegetables.
5. Don't forget the **pot** for boiling soup.
6. Yes, and we need to prepare **forks** and **spoons** too.
7. After that, we'll store the leftovers in the **refrigerator**.
8. If we're making bread, we'll need a **toaster** as well.
9. Perfect, everything's ready!

♣ Thai MasterChef introduced ancient royal recipes to the public for the first time.

วันที่ 74: การแพทย์และสุขภาพ ภาค 2 ✎

1. ฉันไข้และไอ.
2. คุณควรไปคลินิก.
3. แต่ฉันยังปวดหัวและปวดฟัน.
4. คุณอาจจะต้องกินเม็ดยาและดื่มของเหลว.
5. ฉันต้องไปร้านขายยาหรือไม่?
6. ใช่, และอย่าลืมเอาใบสั่งยาไปด้วย.
7. ถ้าฉันแพ้เม็ดยาล่ะ?
8. บอกหมอที่คลินิกเรื่องนี้ด้วยนะ.

✤ In Thai, verbs related to feeling or being, like "to be sick" (ป่วย), don't need an object to make sense.

1. chạn **khị̂** læa 'āi.
2. khun khwār pai **khlīnik**.
3. tæ̀ chạn yang **pūat h̄ụa** læa **pūat fan**.
4. khun 'āc cà tông kin **met yā** læa deūm **khǒng lheūa**.
5. chạn t̂xng pai **r̂ān khāy yā** h̄rụ̄x mị̀?
6. chì, læa ỳā lūem 'ao **bị̂ s̄ạng yā** pai dūay.
7. thả chạn **phæ̂** met yā l̀æ?
8. b̀xk h̄mǒ thī **khlīnik** rê̄ụng nī dūay ná.

1. I'm **feverish** and **coughing**.
2. You should go to a **clinic**.
3. But I also have a **headache** and **toothache**.
4. You might need to take some **pills** and drink **fluids**.
5. Do I need to go to a **pharmacy**?
6. Yes, and don't forget to bring your **prescription**.
7. What if I'm **allergic** to the pills?
8. Tell the doctor at the **clinic** about this too.

✤ In Thailand, motorcycle taxi drivers became public health heroes by delivering food and medicine to COVID-19 patients during lockdowns.

วันที่ 75: การศึกษาและการเรียนรู้ 🌱

1. **นักเรียน** ครับ **ครู** วันนี้เรามีการบ้านอะไรบ้างครับ?
2. วันนี้ต้องทำ**บทเรียน**วิชาประวัติศาสตร์และ**วิชา**คณิตศาสตร์นะ
3. ครับ แล้วเราต้องใช้**หนังสือ**เล่มไหนบ้างครับ?
4. ใช้**หนังสือ**ที่ฉันแจกใน**โรงเรียน**เมื่อวานนี้ และอย่าลืมเขียนด้วย**ปากกา**
5. ครับ ถ้าเรามีคำถาม เราสามารถถาม**ครู**ได้ไหมครับ?
6. ได้สิ ฉันอยู่ที่นี่เพื่อช่วยเหลือ**นักเรียน**ทุกคน
7. ครับ และ**การสอบ**ครั้งถัดไปเมื่อไหร่ครับ?
8. **การสอบ**จะมีในสัปดาห์หน้า อย่าลืมเตรียมตัวให้พร้อมนะ
9. ครับ ขอบคุณครับ **ครู**

✤ In Thai, to express reflexivity, we add "ตัวเอง" (tua-eng) after the verb, meaning "oneself."

1. **nakrīan** khrap **khrū** wan nī rao mī **kān bān** àrai bāng khrap?
2. wan nī tông tham **bột rīan** wíchā prawătthīsāt læa **wíchā** khanitthasāt ná
3. khrap læa rao tông chāi **nangsū** lēm nāi bāng khrap?
4. chāi **nangsū** thī chăn jæk nai **rōngrīan** mēūa wan nī læa yà lâm khīan dūai **pākkā**
5. khrap thâ rao mī kham thăm rao sămāt thăm **khrū** dâi mǎi khrap?
6. dâi sĭ chăn yồ thī nî phŭa chūai lēūa **nakrīan** thuk khon
7. khrap læa **kān sōp** kráng thât dai mēūa rāi khrap?
8. **kān sōp** că mī nai săpdāhāp nâ yà lûm trēm tua hai phrōm ná
9. khrap khộpkhūn khrap **khrū**

1. **Student:** Sir, what homework do we have today?
2. Today, you need to do the **history lesson** and **mathematics**.
3. **Student:** Which **books** do we need to use, sir?
4. Use the **books** I distributed in **school** yesterday, and don't forget to write with a **pen**.
5. **Student:** Sir, if we have questions, can we ask the **teacher**?
6. Of course, I'm here to help all **students**.
7. **Student:** And when is the next **exam**, sir?
8. The **exam** will be next week. Don't forget to prepare well.
9. **Student:** Thank you, sir **Teacher**.

✤ In Thailand, some schools use meditation as a tool for improving students' focus and learning efficiency.

วันที่ 76: เงินและการช็อปปิ้ง 2

1. เครื่องเบิกเงินอัตโนมัติ อยู่ที่ไหนคะ?
2. อยู่ตรงข้ามธนาคารครับ. คุณต้องการใช้ **บัตรเครดิต** หรือ **เงินสด** ครับ?
3. ฉันต้องการใช้ **เงินสด** ค่ะ. แล้ว **อัตราแลกเปลี่ยน** ดีไหมคะ?
4. ตอนนี้ **อัตราแลกเปลี่ยน** ไม่แพงครับ. คุณมี **ใบเสร็จ** จากการช็อปปิ้งไหมครับ?
5. มีค่ะ. แต่ฉันต้องการ **การคืนเงิน** สำหรับสินค้าที่ **แพง** เกินไป.
6. คุณสามารถไปที่เคาน์เตอร์บริการลูกค้าได้ครับ. พวกเขาจะช่วยเรื่อง **การคืนเงิน** ให้คุณ.
7. ขอบคุณค่ะ. แล้ว **ราคา** สินค้าที่ **ถูก** ล่ะคะ?
8. สินค้าที่ **ถูก** มักจะอยู่ในส่วนโปรโมชั่นครับ. คุณสามารถหาได้ใกล้กับทางเข้า.
9. ขอบคุณมากค่ะ.

✤ In Thai, to express the concept of doing something for each other, we add "กัน" (kan) after the verb.

1. **khrèxng bèk ngoen attonomatî** yù thîi nǎi kha?
2. yù trong khâm thanākhān khrap. khun tôngkān chái **bat kradît** rěu **ngoensot** khrap?
3. chǎn tôngkān chái **ngoensot** khâ. láew **attrā lāek plìan** dī mǎi kha?
4. tonní **attrā lāek plìan** mâi phæng khrap. khun mī **bai sèt** jàk kān chóppíng mǎi khrap?
5. mī khâ. tè chǎn tôngkān **kān khūen ngoen** sǎmráp sinphā thâi **phæng** kōen tôo.
6. khun sǎmát pai thîi khaothên bōrihān lūukkhá dâi khrap. phuak khǎo chà wîang **kān khūen ngoen** hâi khun.
7. khôpkhun khâ. láew **rākhā** sinphā thîi **thùk** lâ kha?
8. sinphā thîi **thùk** mák jà yù nai sàwn promōchōn khrap. khun sǎmát hǎa dâi klâi gàp thāng khâo.
9. khôpkhun mâk khâ.

1. Where is the **ATM** located?
2. It's across from the bank. Do you want to use a **credit card** or **cash**?
3. I want to use **cash**. How about the **exchange rate**? Is it good?
4. The **exchange rate** is not expensive right now. Do you have a **receipt** from shopping?
5. Yes, I do. But I want a **refund** for items that were too **expensive**.
6. You can go to the customer service counter. They will help you with the **refund**.
7. Thank you. And what about the **price** of **cheaper** items?
8. **Cheaper** items are usually in the promotion section. You can find it near the entrance.
9. Thank you very much.

✤ In Thailand, the beloved King Bhumibol Adulyadej was not only a monarch but also a jazz musician whose compositions contributed to the country's cultural and economic landscape.

วันที่ 77: กินข้าวนอกบ้าน ภาค 2

1. สวัสดีครับ มาที่ร้านอาหารนี้ครั้งแรกเหรอครับ?
2. ใช่ค่ะ อยากดูเมนูหน่อยค่ะ
3. ครับ มีอาหารเรียกน้ำย่อย และอาหารจานหลัก ครับ
4. มีสลัดกับแซนด์วิชไหมคะ?
5. มีครับ และยังมีขนมปังปิ้งกับแยมด้วยครับ
6. ดีจัง จะลองขนมปังปิ้งกับแยมค่ะ แล้วมีของหวานอะไร
   บ้างคะ?
7. มีช็อกโกแลตครับ อร่อยมากครับ
8. โอเคค่ะ ขอนั่นด้วยแล้วกันค่ะ
9. ครับ รอสักครู่นะครับ

✤ In Thai, to say someone makes someone else do something, use the structure "ให้ (hâi) + person + verb."

1. sawatdī khrap mā thī **rān'āhān** nî khrang ræk hěr'khrap?
2. chāi khà yàk dū **mēnū** ṅxy khà
3. khrap mī **'āhān rīak nāmỳxy** læa **'āhān jān lāk** khrap
4. mī **salat** kap **sændwích** mãi khá?
5. mī khrap læa yang mī **khanom pang pīng** kap **yæm** dūay khrap
6. dī jang cà lộng **khanom pang pīng** kap **yæm** khà læaw mī **khǒng wǎn** 'arai
   bāng khá?
7. mī **chǒkkolæt** khrap 'aɾxy māk khrap
8. o khe khà khǒ nán dūay læaw kan khà
9. khrap rộ sàk khrů̄ ná khrap

1. Hello! Is this your first time at our **restaurant**?
2. Yes, I'd like to see the **menu** please.
3. Sure, we have **appetizers** and **main dishes**.
4. Do you have **salads** and **sandwiches**?
5. Yes, we do. And we also have **toast** with **jam**.
6. Great, I'll try the **toast** with **jam**. What **desserts** do you have?
7. We have **chocolate**, it's really delicious.
8. Okay, I'll have that too, please.
9. Sure, just a moment, please.

✤ In Thailand, the ancient city of Ayutthaya, once destroyed by war, has been meticulously restored, allowing traditional Thai culture and architecture to flourish once again.

วันที่ 78 : บ้านและเฟอร์นิเจอร์ 2 ✒

1. ฉันอยากซื้อ**โซฟา**ใหม่
2. ทำไมล่ะ?
3. **โซฟา**เก่าของฉันเสียแล้ว และฉันก็อยากได้**เตียง**ใหม่ด้วย
4. เราไปดูที่ร้านขาย**เฟอร์นิเจอร์**กันไหม?
5. ดีมาก ฉันยังอยากดู**ตู้เย็น**และ**เตาอบ**ด้วย
6. อย่าลืมดู**โคมไฟ**สวยๆ และ**โทรทัศน์**ใหม่นะ
7. ใช่ ฉันอยากเปลี่ยน**หน้าต่าง**และ**ประตู**ใหม่ด้วย
8. เยี่ยมมาก เราจะได้เฟอร์นิเจอร์ที่ดีที่สุด
9. แล้วเราก็จะไปกินอาหารที่**ร้านอาหาร**หลังจากนั้น

✤ In Thai, to say you do something with an object, like "write with a pen," place the word "**ด้วย**" (dûay) after the object to indicate it's used as an instrument.

1. chạn xyāk sụ̄ **sōfā** mị̀
2. thảmị lạ?
3. **sōfā** kāo k̄hxng chạn s̄īa læ̂w læ chạn k̆ xyāk dị̂ **tīyng** mị̀ d̂wy
4. rāo pị dū thī̀ r̂ān k̄hāy **feụ̄xrnijexr̒** kan mị?
5. dī māk chạn yang xyāk dū **tû̂yen** læ **tā ox** d̂wy
6. xyā lụm dū **khom lạı** s̄wy s̄wy læ **thōrthạs̄̒n** mị̀ ṇa
7. chı̀ chạn xyāk plī̀yan **n̂ātāng** læ **pratū** mị̀ d̂wy
8. yīem māk rāo cā dị̂ feụ̄xrnijexr̒ thī̀ dī thī̀ s̄ud
9. læ̂w rāo cā pị kin 'āh̄ār thī̀ **r̂ān 'āh̄ār** lạngcāk ṇạn

1. I want to buy a new **sofa**.
2. Why is that?
3. My old **sofa** is broken, and I also want a new **bed**.
4. Shall we go look at a **furniture** store?
5. Great idea. I also want to check out **refrigerators** and **ovens**.
6. Don't forget to look at some beautiful **lamps** and a new **television**.
7. Yes, I want to replace the **windows** and **doors** too.
8. Awesome, we'll get the best furniture.
9. And then we can go eat at a **restaurant** after that.

✤ In ancient Thai architecture, homes were often built on stilts to protect against flooding and wild animals, influencing modern Thai interior design with elevated living spaces.

วันที่ 79: สภาพอากาศ II

1. วันนี้อากาศอย่างไรบ้าง?
2. **พยากรณ์**บอกว่าจะมี**พายุ**ค่ะ.
3. จริงเหรอ? ฉันได้ยินว่าอาจจะมี**ฟ้าร้อง**และ**ฟ้าผ่า**ด้วย.
4. ใช่, และอาจจะมี**พายุเฮอริเคน**หรือ**พายุทอร์นาโด**เลยทีเดียว.
5. น่ากลัวจัง! เราควรทำอย่างไร?
6. ควรอยู่ในบ้าน, ปิด**หน้าต่าง**, และติดตามข่าว**พยากรณ์อากาศ**อย่างใกล้ชิด.
7. ถ้าเกิด**แผ่นดินไหว**หรือ**ภูเขาไฟ**ระเบิดล่ะ?
8. ต้องมีแผนอพยพและรู้จักที่ปลอดภัยในบ้านค่ะ.
9. ขอบคุณนะ, ฉันจะจำไว้.

✤ In Thai, to describe when something happens due to the weather, place the adverbial phrase of time or reason at the beginning of the sentence.

1. wannī **ākās** yàngrai bāng?
2. **phayākǭn** bøk wā cà mī **phāyū** khà.
3. cīngrě? chǎn dāiyin wā 'āc cà mī **fā r̂xng** læ **fā phā** dūay.
4. chî, læ 'āc cà mī **phāyū heūrikhen** rěu **phāyū thxnādō** leīydǐdǐaw.
5. nǎ klūa cang! rao khūan thǎngyāngrai?
6. khūan yũ nı bān, pid **n̂ātāng**, læ tīd tām khāo **phayākǭn** **'ākās** yàngrai klìd chid.
7. thǎ s̄kěd **phæn din h̄ıw** rěu **phū khæo fj** ræbıd l̀ā?
8. t̂xng mī phæn 'phyph læ rûcạk thī plxd phạy nı bān khà.
9. khxbkhum ná, chǎn cà cảm wái.

1. How's the **weather** today?
2. The **forecast** says there will be a **storm**.
3. Really? I heard there might be **thunder** and **lightning** too.
4. Yes, and there might even be a **hurricane** or a **tornado**.
5. That's scary! What should we do?
6. We should stay indoors, close the **windows**, and closely follow the **weather forecast**.
7. What if there's an **earthquake** or a **volcano** eruption?
8. We need to have an evacuation plan and know the safe places in the house.
9. Thank you, I'll remember that.

✤ In Thailand, hearing a gecko's call before leaving the house is believed to predict rain.

วันที่ 80: งานอดิเรกและงานอดิเรก II 🌿

1. วันนี้เราจะไปเดินป่ากันไหม?
2. ฉันอยากไปว่ายน้ำมากกว่า แต่ถ้าอากาศชื้นเราไปสโนว์บอร์ดดีกว่า
3. หลังจากนั้นเราจะไปซูเปอร์มาร์เก็ตซื้อเสื้อแจ็คเก็ตใหม่ไหม?
4. ดีมาก! แล้วเราจะไปร้านอาหารทานอาหารจานหลักและของหวาน
5. ฉันอยากลองเมนูใหม่ในร้านนั้น พวกเขามีดนตรีสดด้วย
6. แล้วเย็นนี้เราดูภาพยนตร์หรือละครดี?
7. ภาพยนตร์ดีกว่า ฉันอยากเห็นการเต้นรำและการแสดงในหนัง

✤ In Thai, to express the duration of a leisure activity, place the time duration after the verb and the object.

1. Wan nîʹ rao cà pāi **doēn pà** kan mị?
2. Chạn xỳàk pāi **wâi nám** māk kwà tæ̀ thâ xākāt **chụ̄n** rao pāi **snô bxd** dī kwà
3. Lạng cāk nán rao cà pāi **sû phēr māř kèt** sū̄ **seū̄x jæk kèt** mị̀ mị?
4. Dī māk! Læw rao cà pāi **rán ʻāhān** thān ʻāhān cān lạk læ **khxng hwān**
5. Chạn xỳàk **lxxng me nū̄** mị̀ nı rán nán phūak khæo mī **dontrī** sot dūay
6. Læw yen nîʹ rao dū **phāph ynť** rǣ **lā khr** dī?
7. **Phāph ynť** dī kwà chạn xỳàk **h̄ĕn kān tên rām** læ **kān s̄dæng** nı nạng

1. Are we going **hiking** today?
2. I'd rather go **swimming**, but if it's **humid**, snowboarding would be better.
3. After that, shall we go to the **supermarket** to buy a new **jacket**?
4. Great! Then we'll go to a **restaurant** for **main dishes** and **desserts**.
5. I want to try the **menu** at that place; they have live **music** too.
6. So, shall we watch a **movie** or a **play** tonight?
7. A **movie** would be better. I want to see the **dancing** and **performances** in the film.

✤ In Thailand, bird singing competitions are a cherished hobby, attracting enthusiasts who train their birds to sing beautifully for prestigious titles.

CHALLENGE NO. 8

SPEAK ONLY IN THAI FOR AN HOUR.

ภาษาหลายหลายเป็นสมบัติของมนุษยชาติ

Linguistic diversity is humanity's treasure.

วันที่ 81: การขนส่ง ภาค 2

1. วันนี้เราจะไปที่ไหนดี?
2. อยากไป**เดินป่า**มั้ย?
3. ดีมาก! เราจะไปด้วย**รถยนต์**หรือ**รถไฟ**?
4. คิดว่า**รถไฟ**สะดวกกว่า เราไม่ต้องเหนื่อยขับ**รถยนต์**.
5. แต่ถ้าเราอยากหยุดดู**หน้าต่าง**ระหว่างทางล่ะ?
6. อืม, ถ้าอย่างนั้น**รถยนต์**ดีกว่า. เราสามารถหยุดได้ตามที่เราอยาก.
7. หลังจากเดินป่า เราจะไป**ว่ายน้ำ**ที่เรือ**ใหญ่**ไหม?
8. น่าสนุกดี! แต่อย่าลืมเตรียม**เก้าอี้**พกพาสำหรับพักผ่อนด้วยนะ.
9. แน่นอน! แล้วเจอกันที่**รถยนต์**ในอีกยี่สิบห้านาทีนะ.

✤ In Thai, to indicate where something happens, place the adverbial of place after the verb, like "ไป (go) โรงเรียน (school)" becomes "ไปโรงเรียน" for "go to school."

1. Wan nî ráo cà pāi thî năi dī?
2. Yàak pāi **doen pâ** mái?
3. Dī mâak! Ráo cà pāi dûay **rót yon** rěu **rót fai**?
4. Khít wâa **rót fai** sà-dwàk kwàa. Ráo mâi tông nùeay khàp **rót yon**.
5. Dtàe thâa ráo yàak yùt dū **nâa tàang** rá-wàng thaang là?
6. Êum, thâa yàang nán **rót yon** dī kwàa. Ráo săa-mâat yùt dâi tâam thî ráo yàak.
7. Lăng câak doen pâ ráo cà pāi **wâai nám** thî **reua yài** măi?
8. Nâa sà-nùk dī! Dtàe yàa lêum triam **gâo I** phók phaa săm-ràp phák phôn dûay ná.
9. Àe náwn! Láew jêo kan thî **rót yon** nai èek yîi sìp hâa nâa thî ná.

218

1. Where should we go today?
2. Do you want to go **hiking**?
3. Great! Should we go by **car** or **train**?
4. I think the **train** is more convenient. We won't have to tire ourselves out driving a **car**.
5. But what if we want to stop and look out the **window** along the way?
6. Hmm, in that case, a **car** is better. We can stop wherever we want.
7. After hiking, shall we go **swimming** at the **big boat**?
8. Sounds fun! But don't forget to bring a **portable chair** for resting.
9. Of course! See you at the **car** in twenty-five minutes then.

✤ In Thailand, the tuk-tuk, originally a rickshaw pulled by humans, evolved into a motorized three-wheeler, becoming an iconic symbol of Thai transportation.

วันที่ 82: ธรรมชาติและภูมิศาสตร์ 2 ✎

1. วันนี้เราจะไป**ภูเขา**ไหม?
2. ฉันอยากไป**แม่น้ำ**มากกว่า
3. แต่**มหาสมุทร**ก็สวยนะ
4. ใช่ แต่ฉันชอบ**ทะเลสาบ**มากกว่า**ทะเลทราย**
5. เราควรไป**ป่าดิบชื้น**หรือ**ป่า**ธรรมดา?
6. ฉันคิดว่า**หาดทราย**น่าสนใจกว่า
7. แล้ว**หุบเขา**ล่ะ? มันเงียบสงบ
8. ถ้าเรามีเวลา เราควรไป**เกาะ**ด้วย

✤ In Thai, to express the cause of an action, we use the word "เพราะ" (because) before the reason.

1. Wan nîi ráo cà pai **phūkhao** mǎi?
2. Chǎn yàak pai **mâenam** mâak kwà
3. Tæ̀ **mahāsmuthr** gô s̄wy ná
4. Chî tæ̀ chǎn chôp **thalessāp** mâak kwà **thalaitrāy**
5. Ráo khwām pai **pādīpchūn** rěu **pā** thamadā?
6. Chǎn khit wâ **hādthrāy** nâa sǒn čhàng kwà
7. Lǽo **hūpkhao** là? Man ngīap sōngpōp
8. Thâ ráo mî welā ráo khwām pai **kò** dûay

1. Are we going to the **mountains** today?
2. I'd rather go to the **river**.
3. But the **ocean** is beautiful too.
4. Yes, but I prefer **lakes** over **deserts**.
5. Should we visit the **rainforest** or a regular **forest**?
6. I think the **beach** is more interesting.
7. What about **valleys**? They're peaceful.
8. If we have time, we should also visit an **island**.

✤ In Thailand, the enchanting Khao Sok National Park is home to one of the world's oldest rainforests, older even than the Amazon.

วันที่ 83: เวลาและกิจวัตรประจำ 🎵

1. **เมื่อวาน** เราไป **เดินป่า** ที่ภูเขา
2. จริงเหรอ? **วันนี้** คุณจะทำอะไร
3. **วันนี้** ฉันจะไป **ว่ายน้ำ** ที่แม่น้ำ
4. ดีจัง! **พรุ่งนี้** ล่ะ?
5. **พรุ่งนี้** ฉันคิดจะอยู่บ้าน ทำอาหาร **เที่ยง** และ **เย็น**
6. **ตอนนี้** คุณหิวไหม?
7. ไม่นะ, แต่ฉันจะทำข้าว **เช้า** พรุ่งนี้
8. คุณใช้ **กระทะ** หรือ **เตาอบ**?
9. ฉันใช้ **กระทะ** สำหรับทำไข่ดาว

✤ In Thai, to express the purpose of an action, we often use "เพื่อ" (pêua) before the verb that describes the purpose.

1. **Mừa wān** rao pai **doēn pà** thỉ phūkhao
2. Cing ro? **Wan nî** khun ca tham arai
3. **Wan nî** chan ca pai **wâi nám** thỉ mænam
4. Dī cang! **Phrung nî** la?
5. **Phrung nî** chan khit ca yû̀ bān tham āhān **thīang** læa **yen**
6. **Ton nî** khun hıw hịm?
7. Mị̀ ná, tæ̀ chan ca tham khāo **chāo** phrung nî
8. Khun chî **krathā** rū̀ **tao op**?
9. Chan chî **krathā** s̄āmhrạb tham khài dāo

1. **Yesterday**, I went **hiking** in the mountains.
2. Really? **Today**, what are you going to do?
3. **Today**, I'm going to **swim** in the river.
4. That's great! What about **tomorrow**?
5. **Tomorrow, I plan to stay at home, cook lunch and dinner**.
6. **Right now**, are you hungry?
7. No, but I will make breakfast **tomorrow** morning.
8. Do you use a **pan** or an **oven**?
9. I use a **pan** for frying eggs.

✤ In Thailand, many locals start their day with a traditional offering of food to monks during their morning alms round.

วันที่ 84: อารมณ์ III ✎

1. เมื่อวานฉัน**กังวล**มาก แต่ตอนนี้ฉันรู้สึก**ผ่อนคลาย**
2. จริงหรือ? เมื่อวานฉันก็**หงุดหงิด**เพราะ**ปวดหัว**
3. วันนี้เช้าฉัน**พอใจ**กับการทำงานมาก
4. ฉันก็**ภูมิใจ**ในตัวเองเหมือนกัน เพราะเมื่อคืนทำงานเสร็จ
   ทันเวลา
5. แต่ฉันยังคงรู้สึก**กลัว**เรื่องการนัดหมายพรุ่งนี้
6. ไม่ต้อง**กังวล** ฉันเชื่อว่าทุกอย่างจะเป็นไปด้วยดี
7. ขอบคุณนะ คำพูดของเธอทำให้ฉัน**ปลื้มปีติ**
8. ฉันหวังว่าเราทั้งคู่จะไม่รู้สึก**เดียวดาย**อีกต่อไป
9. ใช่ มีเพื่อนอย่างเธอ ฉันไม่**โกรธ**หรือ**กระวนกระวาย**เลย

✤ In Thai, to describe someone's emotion using a relative clause, you place the emotion word after the person and use "ที่" (thîi) to connect the description, like "เด็กที่มีความสุข" (the child who is happy).

1. Mũa wān chạn **kangwon** māk tæ̀ tǫnnî chạn rûsuk **p̀hxn klāy**
2. Cing rŭ? Mũa wān chạn k̂ĥ **hngudhngid** phrā **pūad h̄ụạ**
3. Wạṅ nî chā chạn **phǿcı** kạb kār thamngān māk
4. Chạn k̂ĥ **phūmịcı** nı tạw eng mừngkan phrā mũa khnî thamngān s̄ŕc thạn wēlā
5. Tæ̀ chạn yang khong rûsuk **klūa** rừxng kār nạd h̄māy phrûngnî
6. Mị̀ t̂xng **kangwon** chạn chụ̀x wā thuk xyāng cā pen pāi dı dī
7. K̂hxbkhuṇ ná kham phūd k̂hxng theū thâh̄î chạn **plūm pīt**
8. Chạn h̄wạng wā rao thạng khū̀ cā mị̀ rûsuk **dīyw dāy** xīk t̀ā pị
9. Cì mī pheụ̀xn xyāng theū chạn mị̀ **kroth** rǽu **krāwn krāwy** leū̄xy

224

1. Yesterday, I was **worried** a lot, but now I feel **relaxed**.
2. Really? Yesterday, I was also **irritated** because of a **headache**.
3. This morning, I am very **satisfied** with my work.
4. I am also **proud** of myself because I finished my work on time last night.
5. But I still feel **scared** about the appointment tomorrow.
6. Don't **worry**. I believe everything will be fine.
7. Thank you. Your words make me feel **delighted**.
8. I hope both of us will no longer feel **lonely**.
9. Yes, having a friend like you, I don't feel **angry** or **anxious** at all.

✤ In Thailand, the Loi Krathong Festival is celebrated by floating decorated baskets on water to honor the water spirits and symbolize the release of negative emotions and grudges.

วันที่ 85: สีและรูปทรง 🥄

1. วันนี้เรามีบทเรียนอะไรบ้าง?
2. มีวิชาพาสต้า ครูให้ทำการบ้านเกี่ยวกับสีและรูปทรงด้วย.
3. จริงเหรอ? เราต้องใช้สีอะไรบ้าง?
4. แดง, น้ำเงิน, เขียว, เหลือง, ดำ, ขาว, เทา, และชมพู.
5. แล้วรูปทรงล่ะ?
6. ต้องมีกลมและสี่เหลี่ยม.
7. ฉันพอใจกับการบ้านนี้นะ.
8. ฉันก็เหมือนกัน ชอบทำอาหาร และชอบใช้เนยและพริก
   ไทยในพาสต้า.
9. ดีจัง! เรามาทำกันเถอะ.

✤ In Thai, to combine colors and shapes in a sentence, use the conjunction "และ" (láe)
meaning "and" to link them together.

1. Wan nî rao mī bŏt rīan àrai bāng?
2. Mī wíchā pā̄stā khrū hî tham kān b̂ān k̀ỳw kàp s̄ī læa rūp throng dūay.
3. Cìngrĕo? Rao t̂xng chái s̄ī àrai bāng?
4. Daeng, n̂āngin, k̄hīaw, l̂heǖxng, dam, k̄hāw, thæo, læa chomphū.
5. Læa rūp throng l̀ā?
6. T̂xng mī klom læa s̄ì lìam.
7. Chạn phx cĥī kàp kān b̂ān nī ná.
8. Chạn k̄ĥ mæng kan chxb tham āhān læa chxb chái neīy læa phrik thai nı
   pā̄stā.
9. Dī cạng! Rao mā tham kan t̀ĕ.

226

1. What do we have for **lessons** today?
2. We have **Pasta class**. The teacher assigned **homework** related to **colors** and **shapes** as well.
3. Really? What **colors** do we need to use?
4. **Red, Blue, Green, Yellow, Black, White, Grey**, and **Pink**.
5. And what about the **shapes**?
6. We need **circles** and **squares**.
7. I'm **pleased** with this homework.
8. Me too, I love cooking and using **butter** and **pepper** in **pasta**.
9. Great! Let's do it together.

✤ In Thai art, the lotus shape symbolizes purity and enlightenment, deeply rooted in Buddhist beliefs.

วันที่ 86: ความสัมพันธ์ 🌱

1. วันนี้เป็นวันอะไร?
2. วันนี้วันพุธครับ.
3. คุณมีแผนทำอะไรกับ**ครอบครัว**หรือ**เพื่อน**บ้างไหม?
4. ผมจะไปดูหนังกับ**เพื่อนร่วมงาน**ตอนเย็นครับ.
5. สนุกดีนะ คุณจะใช้**เงินสด**หรือ**บัตรเครดิต**จ่าย?
6. ผมคิดว่าจะใช้**บัตรเครดิต**ครับ.
7. แล้วพรุ่งนี้ล่ะ มีแผนอะไร?
8. พรุ่งนี้ผมจะไปเยี่ยม**ญาติ**ที่บ้านครับ.
9. ดีมากเลย ขอให้สนุกกับการพบปะ**ครอบครัว**และ**เพื่อน**นะ
   ครับ.

✤ In Thai, to express when something happens in relation to another action, we use the word "เมื่อ" (mûea) at the beginning of an adverbial clause, like "เมื่อฉันไปถึงบ้าน" (mûea chăn bpai têung bâan) meaning "when I arrive at home".

1. Wannî pen wan 'arai?
2. Wannî wan phut khrap.
3. Khun mī phæn tham 'arai kap **khrǭpkhrua** rǔ **phǔn** bāng h̆ǐm?
4. Phǒm cà pāi du năng kap **phǔn rûamngān** tawn yen khrap.
5. Sanuk dī ná khun cà chái **ngœn sot** rǔ **bạt krēdit** cāi?
6. Phǒm khid wâ cà chái **bạt krēdit** khrap.
7. Læa phrûngnî lạ mī phæn 'arai?
8. Phrûngnî phǒm cà pai yîam **yāti** thî̆ bān khrap.
9. Dī māk lœi khǭ h̆ị̆ sanuk kap kān phobpha **khrǭpkhrua** læa **phǔn** ná khrap.

228

1. What day is it today?
2. Today is Wednesday.
3. Do you have any plans with your **family** or **friends**?
4. I'm going to the movies with **coworkers** this evening.
5. That sounds fun. Will you be paying with **cash** or a **credit card**?
6. I think I'll use a **credit card**.
7. What about tomorrow? Any plans?
8. Tomorrow, I'm going to visit **relatives** at their home.
9. That's great. Have a good time with your **family** and **friends**.

✤ In Thai literature, the epic tale of "Khun Chang Khun Phaen" explores the complexities of love and friendship through a tragic love triangle that has captivated readers for centuries.

วันที่ 87: เสื้อผ้าและเครื่องประดับ ✑

1. วันนี้เราจะไปซื้อ**เสื้อผ้า**กันไหม?
2. อยากได้**เสื้อแจ็คเก็ต**และ**รองเท้า**ใหม่ค่ะ.
3. เราก็อยากได้**หมวก**กับ**แว่นตากันแดด**นะ.
4. แล้วคุณล่ะ? ชอบ**เสื้อ**หรือ**กางเกง**?
5. ฉันชอบ**กระโปรง**มากกว่า แต่ก็อยากได้**สร้อยคอ**สวยๆ ด้วย.
6. ฉันคิดว่า**ต่างหู**คู่ใหม่ก็จะดีนะ.
7. ใช่เลย, ซื้อกันเถอะ!

✤ In Thai, to compare two items of clothing, use "กว่า" (gwà) after the adjective, like "เสื้อนี้ สวยกว่า" (sûea níi sǔay gwà) meaning "This shirt is prettier."

1. Wanní rao cà pāi séu**sêûaphâ** kan mị?
2. Yàk dâi **sêûa jæk kèt** læ **rông tháo** mài khà.
3. Rao kộ yàk dâi **mùak** kàp **wæ̀n tā kan dæd** ná.
4. Léao khun lè? Chôb **sêûa** rǔ **kāngken**?
5. Chạn chôb **kràprōng** māk kwà chà kộ yàk dâi **sr̂xy kha** s̄wy s̄wy dûay.
6. Chạn khíd wâ **tàeng hū** khǔ mài kộ cà dī ná.
7. Chài leo, séû kan thò!

1. Are we going shopping for **clothes** today?
2. I want a new **jacket** and **shoes**.
3. I'd like a **hat** and **sunglasses** too.
4. What about you? Do you prefer **shirts** or **pants**?
5. I prefer **skirts**, but I also want a beautiful **necklace**.
6. I think a new pair of **earrings** would be nice too.
7. Absolutely, let's go shopping!

✤ In ancient Thailand, the length of a person's fingernails indicated their social status, with long nails signifying nobility and a life free from manual labor.

วันที่ 88: เทคโนโลยีและสื่อ 2 🎋

1. เธอดู**โทรทัศน์**ช่องไหนอยู่?
2. ฉันดูข่าวอยู่ที่ช่องสาม. แล้วเธอล่ะ?
3. ฉันชอบฟัง**วิทยุ**มากกว่า. มันสบายดี.
4. เธอได้ยินข่าวล่าสุดจาก**วิทยุ**หรือเปล่า?
5. ไม่นะ, ฉันติดตามข่าวใน**โซเชียลมีเดีย**มากกว่า.
6. ฉันก็เหมือนกัน. ฉันใช้**สมาร์ทโฟน**เช็คข่าว**ออนไลน์**.
7. แล้วเธอใช้**คอมพิวเตอร์**สำหรับงานหรือเปล่า?
8. ใช่, แต่ฉันก็ส่ง**อีเมล**และทำงานผ่าน**สมาร์ทโฟน**ได้ด้วย.
9. สะดวกจริงๆ นะ, เทคโนโลยีสมัยนี้.

✤ In Thai, to express a cause, use "**เพราะ**" (because) at the beginning of a sentence, followed by the reason, and then the result.

1. Thœ̌ du **thōrathat** chǿng nǎi yū?
2. Chǎn du khāo yū thī chǿng sām. Laēo thœ̌ læ?
3. Chǎn chǿp fang **withayu** māk kwā. Man sabāi dī.
4. Thœ̌ dāi yin khāo lāsut cāk **withayu** rǔ plāo?
5. Mai ná, chǎn tit tăm khāo nai **sōchīal mīdīa** māk kwā.
6. Chǎn kǭ mǔan kan. Chǎn chai **smātthōfon** chek khāo **xnlayn**.
7. Laēo thœ̌ chai **khxmphūtœ̌** samrǔp ngān rǔ plāo?
8. Chai, tæ̀ chǎn kǭ sǒng **īmel** læ tham ngān phān **smātthōfon** dāi dūay.
9. Sādūak cing cing ná, thekhnolōyī samai nī.

1. What **TV channel** are you watching?
2. I'm watching the news on channel three. What about you?
3. I prefer listening to the **radio** more. It's quite relaxing.
4. Did you hear the latest news on the **radio**?
5. No, I follow the news more on **social media**.
6. Same here. I use my **smartphone** to check the news **online**.
7. Do you use a **computer** for work?
8. Yes, but I also send **emails** and work through my **smartphone** as well.
9. It's really convenient, isn't it? Technology these days.

✤ In Thailand, the first movie theater was a royal gift from King Chulalongkorn in 1905, marking the beginning of the country's cinematic journey in the era of technological innovation.

วันที่ 89: อาหารและเครื่องดื่ม ภาค 2

1. วันนี้คุณอยากกินเนื้อสัตว์หรือผักคะ?
2. ฉันอยากกินผักมากกว่าครับ.
3. แล้วดื่มอะไรดีคะ? น้ำ, โซดา, หรือน้ำผลไม้?
4. ฉันเลือกน้ำผลไม้ครับ.
5. คุณชอบผลไม้ชนิดไหนในน้ำผลไม้คะ?
6. ฉันชอบมะม่วงครับ.
7. ตกลงค่ะ, แล้วเพื่อนๆ ล่ะ? พวกเขาชอบดื่มเบียร์, ชา, หรือกาแฟ?
8. เพื่อนฉันชอบชาครับ.
9. โอเคค่ะ, ฉันจะเตรียมให้ทุกคนเลยนะคะ.

✤ If you want to eat spicy food in Thailand, you should say "Chan chawb aahaan phet."

1. Wannî khun xỳāk kin **nửa sątử** rửx **phạk** khá?

2. Chạn xỳāk kin **phạk** mākkwà khạb.

3. Lǣw dùem xarī dī khá? **Nả, so dā, rửx nả phl mị**?

4. Chạn lūek **nả phl mị** khạb.

5. Khun chxb **phl mị** chnid ḥịn nı nả phl mị khá?

6. Chạn chxb mā mèung khạb.

7. Toklong khà, lǣw pheụ̂xn pheụ̂xn lạ? Phwk khæo chxb dùem **bīa, chā, rửx kāfæ**?

8. Pheụ̂xn chạn chxb **chā** khạb.

9. Okhê khà, chạn c̄hā trīam ḥî thuk khon loei ná khà.

1. Do you want to eat **meat** or **vegetables** today?
2. I'd prefer **vegetables**.
3. What would you like to drink? **Water, soda, or juice**?
4. I'll go with **juice**.
5. What kind of **fruit** do you like in your juice?
6. I like mango.
7. Alright, and what about your friends? Do they prefer **beer, tea, or coffee**?
8. My friends like **tea**.
9. Okay, I'll prepare everything for everyone then.

✤ In Thailand, the beloved street food dish Pad Thai was actually popularized in the 1930s as part of a campaign to promote Thai nationalism and reduce rice consumption.

วันที่ 90: บ้านและชีวิต ✎

1. **บ้าน** ของเธอมีกี่ **ห้องนอน**?
2. มีสอง **ห้องนอน** หนึ่ง **ห้องน้ำ** และ **ห้องครัว** หนึ่งห้องค่ะ.
3. เธอมี **สวน** หรือ ลาน ไหม?
4. มี **สวน** เล็กๆ ข้าง **บ้าน** ค่ะ.
5. แล้ว **ห้องนั่งเล่น** ล่ะ? ใหญ่ไหม?
6. ไม่ค่อยใหญ่ค่ะ แต่มี **ระเบียง** สวยๆ.
7. เธอชอบทำอะไรใน **บ้าน**?
8. ชอบดู**ภาพยนตร์** และ **ว่ายน้ำ** ที่ **โรงรถ** ที่แปลงเป็นสระค่ะ.

✤ In Thai, to express something that happens before something else, we use "ก่อนที่" (before) followed by the action, and then the main clause.

1. **bān** khāng thǭ mī kī **h̄̒xngnxn**?
2. mī s̄xng **h̄̒xngnxn** nưng **h̄̒ngn̂ām** læa **h̄̒ngkhrūa** nưng h̄̒ng kh̀ā.
3. thǭ mī **s̄wn** rū̄ **lān** mị̀?
4. mī **s̄wn** lĕk̄̂kh̄̒ khāng **bān** kh̀ā.
5. læa **h̄̒ngnạ̀nglĕn** l̀ā? h̄ıỵ̀ mị̀?
6. mị̀ khxy h̄ıỵ̀ kh̀ā tæ̀ mī **rạbīyng** s̄wyỳ.
7. thǭ chxb thả̄rị nı **bān**?
8. chxb dū**p̣hāphyntr̒** læa **ẁāynām** thī **rōngrth** thī̀ pælng pĕn s̄rạ kh̀ā.

236

1. **How many bedrooms** does your house have?
2. It has two **bedrooms**, one **bathroom**, and one **kitchen**.
3. Do you have a **garden** or a **patio**?
4. There's a small **garden** next to the **house**.
5. What about the **living room**? Is it big?
6. Not really, but it has a beautiful **balcony**.
7. What do you like to do at **home**?
8. I enjoy watching **movies** and **swimming** in the **garage** converted into a pool.

✤ In Thailand, the Jim Thompson House, once home to an American silk entrepreneur, is now a museum showcasing his collection of Asian art and his mysterious disappearance.

CHALLENGE NO. 9

WATCH A MOVIE IN THAI WITHOUT ENGLISH SUBTITLES AND SUMMARIZE THE STORY.

ทุกความสำเร็จเล็กๆ น้อยๆ ควรได้รับการฉลอง

Every small success deserves to be celebrated.

วันที่ 91: ช้อปปิ้งและร้านค้า

1. วันนี้เราจะไป**ซูเปอร์มาร์เก็ต**หรือ**ศูนย์การค้า**?
2. ไป**ศูนย์การค้า**ดีกว่า มี**ร้านค้า**เยอะกว่า.
3. อย่าลืมเอา**ตะกร้า**และ**รถเข็น**นะ.
4. ใช่ แล้วเราจะไปจ่ายที่**แคชเชียร์**เมื่อไหร่?
5. เมื่อเราเลือกซื้อของเสร็จสิ. หวังว่าจะมี**ส่วนลด**.
6. ใช่ ฉันอยากได้ของ**ลดราคา**.
7. หลังจากนั้นเราจะได้**ใบเสร็จ**เพื่อตรวจสอบ**ราคา**.
8. ดีมาก ฉันชอบช้อปปิ้งแบบนี้.

✤ In Thai, to describe where something is located while shopping, place the location word after the noun, like "**หนังสืออยู่บนโต๊ะ**" (The book is on the table).

1. Wannî rao cà pāi **sû pe ŕ mār̀ ket̀** r̀eū **s̄ūny kār khā**?

2. Pāi **s̄ūny kār khā** dī kwà mī **r̄ān khā** yeù kwà.

3. Yà lūm ao **takrá** læa **rth khen** ná.

4. Chî læa rao cà pāi càly thî **khaêchchīār̀** mêuā ḥịr̀?

5. Mêuā rao lūek s̄ū kh̄ŏng s̄èt s̄ì. Ḥwạng wâ chā mī **s̄̀ạn lōd**.

6. Chî chạn xỳāk dāi kh̄ŏng **lōd rā khā**.

7. Ḥlạng cāk nán rao cà dāi **bı s̄r̀et̀** pheụ̀x trwc s̄xāb **rā khā**.

8. Dī māk chạn chxb chxbping bæb nî.

1. Today, are we going to the **supermarket** or the **shopping center**?
2. Let's go to the **shopping center**; it has more **stores**.
3. Don't forget to bring the **basket** and **cart**.
4. Right, and when will we go to the **cashier**?
5. After we finish selecting our items. Hopefully, there will be some **discounts**.
6. Yes, I want to get some **discounted items**.
7. After that, we'll get a **receipt** to check the **prices**.
8. Great, I like shopping like this.

✤ In Thailand, floating markets have evolved from traditional community trading spots to major tourist attractions, showcasing the vibrant evolution of retail trade.

วันที่ 92: ฉุกเฉินและความปลอดภัย 🌱

1. **ฉุกเฉิน** ค่ะ! มี**ไฟ**ไหม้!
2. โทรหา**ตำรวจ** และ **รถพยาบาล** ด่วนเลย
3. คุณ**ปลอดภัย**ไหม?
4. ผม**ปลอดภัย**ครับ แต่ต้องการ**ช่วยเหลือ**
5. ผมจะทำ**การปฐมพยาบาล**ให้นะ
6. ขอบคุณครับ แล้วเราจะไป**โรงพยาบาล**ไหม?
7. ใช่ค่ะ ต้องไปให้**แพทย์**ดูอาการ
8. สถานการณ์นี้**อันตราย**มาก
9. ใช่ค่ะ แต่ตอนนี้เรา**ปลอดภัย**แล้ว

✤ In Thai, to express purpose or reason, add "เพื่อ" (pêua) before the verb in the final clause, like "เพื่อความปลอดภัย" (pêua khwam plòt phai) for "for safety".

1. **Chukchœn** khà! Mī **fai** māi!
2. Thǫ rō hā **tamruat** læa **rōt phayābān** dùan loēi
3. Khun **plōdphai** māi?
4. Phǫm **plōdphai** khrap æa t̂xngkān **chuaihelūa**
5. Phǫm čha tham **kān pathomphayābān** h̄ā na
6. Khǭpkhun khrap læa rao čha pai **rōngphayābān** māi?
7. Chai khà t̂xng pai hāi **phæt** dū ākān
8. Sathānakān nī '**antray** māk
9. Chai khà tæa tōnnī rao **plōdphai** lǽo

1. **Emergency**! There's a **fire**!
2. Call the **police** and **ambulance** immediately.
3. Are you **safe**?
4. I'm **safe**, but I need **help**.
5. I'll give you **first aid**.
6. Thank you. Are we going to the **hospital**?
7. Yes, we need to have a **doctor** check you.
8. This situation is very **dangerous**.
9. Yes, but we are **safe** now.

✤ In Thailand, a group of young soccer players and their coach were heroically rescued from a flooded cave by divers in a complex operation that captivated the world.

วันที่ 93: การเดินทางและสถานที่ III 🌴

1. วันนี้คุณมีหนังสือเดินทางกับวีซ่าไหม?

2. มีครับ/ค่ะ และผม/ดิฉันก็ทำการจองที่พักและตั๋วเรียบร้อยแล้ว

3. คุณมีสัมภาระเยอะไหม?

4. ไม่ครับ/ค่ะ ผม/ดิฉันมีแค่กระเป๋าเป้หนึ่งใบและกระเป๋าเดินทางหนึ่งใบ

5. คุณเป็นนักท่องเที่ยวหรือไกด์ครับ/ค่ะ?

6. ผม/ดิฉันเป็นนักท่องเที่ยวครับ/ค่ะ และผม/ดิฉันมีแผนที่ด้วย

7. คุณจะไปสนามบินหรือสถานีรถไฟครับ/ค่ะ?

8. ผม/ดิฉันจะไปสนามบินครับ/ค่ะ เพราะว่าพรุ่งนี้ผม/ดิฉันมีเที่ยวบินตอนเช้า

9. โอเคครับ/ค่ะ ขอให้เดินทางปลอดภัยนะครับ/ค่ะ

✤ Even though it's raining, we can still visit the temple by saying "แม้จะฝนตก เราก็ยังไปวัด
ได้" in Thai.

1. **Wanni̅** khun mī **na̲ngs̄ǔx dein thāng** ka̲b **wīs̄ā** mị̀?

2. Mī khrạb/kh̀ā læa phǒm/dichạn k̄h̀ thả **kār cǒng** thī phạk læa **tạw** rīap rói læw

3. Khun mī **sạmphār** yeụ̀x mị̀?

4. Mị̀ khrạb/kh̀ā phǒm/dichạn mī khæ **krạpǎo pæ̀** nụ̀ng bị læa **krạpǎo dein
   thāng** nụ̀ng bị

5. Khun pen **na̲k thŏngthı̀yw** reụ̀x **kịd** khrạb/kh̀ā?

6. Phǒm/dichạn pen na̲k thŏngthı̀yw khrạb/kh̀ā læa phǒm/dichạn mī **phæn
   thı̄** dūay

7. Khun cà pị **s̄nāmbin** reụ̀x **s̄thānī rthfị** khrạb/kh̀ā?

8. Phǒm/dichạn cà pị **s̄nāmbin** khrạb/kh̀ā phr̀x wâ phrûngni̅ phǒm/dichạn mī
   theı̅ywbin tawn chāo

9. Ok khrạb/kh̀ā k̄hx h̄ı̂ cæn thāng plxd phạy na̲ khrạb/kh̀ā

1. **Do you have your passport and visa today?**
2. Yes, I do. And I've also made reservations for accommodation and tickets.
3. **Do you have a lot of luggage?**
4. No, I just have one backpack and one suitcase.
5. **Are you a tourist or a guide?**
6. I'm a tourist, and I have a map too.
7. **Are you going to the airport or the train station?**
8. I'm going to the airport because I have a flight tomorrow morning.
9. **Okay, have a safe trip!**

✤ The Oriental Hotel in Bangkok, established in 1876, has hosted famous guests like Joseph Conrad and Somerset Maugham, who found inspiration for their novels within its walls.

วันที่ 94: สัตว์และสัตว์เลี้ยง 🌿

1. คุณชอบ**หมา**หรือ**แมว**มากกว่ากัน?
2. ฉันชอบ**แมว**มากกว่า เพราะมันน่ารักและเงียบ.
3. แล้วคุณมี**นก**หรือ**ปลา**เป็นสัตว์เลี้ยงไหม?
4. ไม่, แต่ฉันมี**ม้า**อยู่ที่บ้านนอก.
5. ว้าว! คุณมี**วัว**หรือ**แกะ**ด้วยไหม?
6. ไม่, แต่เรามี**แพะ**และ**ไก่**.
7. ฉันอยากมี**หมู**เป็นสัตว์เลี้ยง.
8. จริงเหรอ? ฉันคิดว่ามันคงทำให้ฉัน**หงุดหงิด**.
9. แต่ฉันคิดว่ามันน่ารักและทำให้ฉัน**ปลื้มปีติ**.

✤ In Thai, to explain or give more information about an animal or pet, we use the word "ที่"
(thîi) before adding the explanatory clause.

1. khun chxb **mā** rū̄ **mæw** māk kwā kạn?

2. chạn chxb **mæw** māk kwā phrā mạn nā rak læa ngīap.

3. læa khun mī **nk** rū̄ **plā** pen ṣạtẇ līyng h̄ịm?

4. mị̀, tæ̀ chạn mī **mā** xyū̄ thī̄ bān nxk.

5. wāw! khun mī **wūa** rū̄ **kæ̀** dūay h̄ịm?

6. mị̀, tæ̀ rao mī **phæ** læa **kị̀**.

7. chạn xỳāk mī **mū** pen ṣạtẇ līyng.

8. cring h̄rụ̄x? chạn khid wā mạn khng thả h̄ịn chạn **hngud hngid**.

9. tæ̀ chạn khid wā mạn nā rak læa thả chạn **plụ̄m pīt**.

1. Do you prefer **dogs** or **cats**?
2. I prefer **cats** because they are cute and quiet.
3. Do you have any **birds** or **fish** as pets?
4. No, but I have a **horse** at my country house.
5. Wow! Do you have any **cows** or **sheep** too?
6. No, but we have **goats** and **chickens**.
7. I would like to have a **pig** as a pet.
8. Really? I think it would just **annoy** me.
9. But I think they're cute and make me **happy**.

✤ In Thailand, the white elephant is revered and considered a symbol of royal power and good fortune.

วันที่ 95: งานและอาชีพ 🌱

1. วันนี้เรามี**การประชุม**ที่**สำนักงาน**ไหม?
2. มีครับ, **เจ้านาย**บอกว่ามี**การนำเสนอ**รายงาน.
3. **พนักงาน**คนใหม่จะเข้าร่วมด้วยไหม?
4. ใช่, **เพื่อนร่วมงาน**ทุกคนจะมา. **กำหนดส่ง**รายงานคือ วันไหน?
5. **กำหนดส่ง**คือวันที่ยี่สิบสอง.
6. โอเค, ฉันต้องเตรียม**การจ้างงาน**ให้เสร็จสิ้น.
7. ถ้าต้องการความช่วยเหลือ, บอกฉันนะ.
8. ขอบคุณมาก. การทำงานร่วมกันช่วยให้งานเสร็จเร็วขึ้น.
9. ใช่, ทำงานร่วมกันดีที่สุด!

✤ In Thai, to quote someone directly, we use the particle "ว่า" (wâa) before the quoted speech, without changing the verb tense.

1. Wannî rao mī **kār prachum** thī **samnakngān** mị?
2. Mī khrap, **chāonāi** bøk wā mī **kār nam s̄eñ'** rāyngān.
3. **Phanakngān** khon mị cā khāo rūm dūay mị?
4. Chî, **pheụ̂xn rūmngān** thuk khon cā mā. **Kamnod s̄̀ng** rāyngān khụ̄x wan nị?
5. **Kamnod s̄̀ng** khụ̄x wan thî yīs̄ips̄̀ng.
6. Ok, chạn t̂xng trīam **kār cāngngān** h̄ı̂ s̄r̂xtsin.
7. Thǎ t̂xngkān khwām ch̀wy h̄elụ̄x, bøk chạn ná.
8. K̄hxbkhuṇ māk. Kār thamngān rūmkan chwy h̄ı̂ ngān s̄r̂xt rew k̄hụ̂n.
9. Chî, thamngān rūmkan dī thîs̄ud!

1. Do we have a **meeting** at the **office** today?
2. Yes, the **boss** said there's a presentation of the report.
3. Will the new **employee** join too?
4. Yes, all **coworkers** will be there. When is the **deadline** for the report?
5. The **deadline** is on the twenty-second.
6. Okay, I need to finish the **hiring process**.
7. If you need help, let me know.
8. Thank you so much. Working together helps to finish the work faster.
9. Yes, teamwork is the best!

✤ In ancient Thailand, royal court astrologers held influential careers, guiding kings on matters of state and war based on celestial events.

วันที่ 96: วันและเดือน 🌱

1. วันนี้วันอะไร?
2. **วันจันทร์** ครับ.
3. แล้วพรุ่งนี้ล่ะ?
4. **วันอังคาร** ครับ.
5. คุณมีแผนอะไรใน **วันพุธ** บ้างไหม?
6. ผมมีการจองตั๋วไปเที่ยวในเดือนมกราคม.
7. สนุกดีนะ! แล้วใน **วันพฤหัสบดี** ล่ะ?
8. ผมต้องไปสำนักงานคุยกับเจ้านาย.
9. โชคดีนะครับ!

✤ In Thai, when changing direct speech to indirect speech about days and months, you often use the word "ว่า" (wâa) to introduce what was said, without changing the tense of the original statement.

1. Wan nî wan à-rai?
2. **Wan can** khrap.
3. Lêo phrûng nî lè?
4. **Wan angkhān** khrap.
5. Khun mī phæn à-rai nai **wan phūt** bāng mǎi?
6. Phǒm mī kān cǒng tūa pai thîaw nai deūan **makarākhom**.
7. Šnuk dī ná! Lêo nai **wan phrūhat šbdi** lè?
8. Phǒm t̂xng pai šāmṇạkngān khuy kàp cêā nāi.
9. Chok dī ná khrap!

1. What day is it today?
2. **Monday**.
3. And what about tomorrow?
4. **Tuesday**.
5. Do you have any plans for **Wednesday**?
6. I have a booking for a trip in **January**.
7. Sounds fun! How about **Thursday**?
8. I have to go to the office to talk with my boss.
9. Good luck!

✤ In ancient Thailand, the lunar calendar was so integral to agriculture and festivals that its months were named after rice farming stages.

วันที่ 97: ร่างกายและสุขภาพ 🌱

1. วันนี้หัวเจ็บมาก
2. ฉันเห็นมือของเธอแดงด้วย
3. ใช่, เท้าก็เจ็บเหมือนกัน
4. **แขนและขาของฉันไม่สบาย**
5. ต้องไปหาหมอไหม?
6. ไม่, ฉันคิดว่าต้องพักผ่อน
7. **ตาของฉันรู้สึกดีขึ้นเมื่อปิด**
8. **หู, จมูก, และปากของฉันไม่มีปัญหา**
9. แต่นิ้วยังเจ็บอยู่

✤ In Thai, to express someone's thoughts or speech indirectly without changing the tense, we often use "ว่า" (wâa) like saying "He said he was tired" becomes "เขาบอกว่าเขาเหนื่อย" (khǎo bòk wâa khǎo nùeay).

1. wan nī**huā** cĕp māk
2. chǎn hēn **mue** khǎng thǒe daeng dūai
3. chaī, **tháo** kǒ cĕp mūran kan
4. **khaen** læ **khā** khǎng chǎn mǎi sàbāi
5. tǒng pai hā mǒ mǎi?
6. mǎi, chǎn khit wā tǒng phák phǒn
7. **tā** khǎng chǎn rū sùk dī khûn mūra pìt
8. **hū, chamūk, læ pāk** khǎng chǎn mǎi mī panhā
9. dtàe **níu** yang cĕp yù

1. Today, my **head** hurts a lot.
2. I see your **hand** is red too.
3. Yes, my **feet** hurt as well.
4. My **arms** and **legs** are feeling unwell.
5. Should we see a doctor?
6. No, I think I need some rest.
7. My **eyes** feel better when closed.
8. My **ears, nose, and mouth** are fine.
9. But my **fingers** still hurt.

♣ In Thailand, the traditional sport of Sepak Takraw, akin to volleyball but using feet instead of hands, showcases the locals' incredible agility and skill.

วันที่ ๙๘: การศึกษาและการเรียนรู้ ๒ 🌱

1. วันนี้เรามี**การบ้าน**เยอะไหม?
2. มีค่ะ แต่ฉันใช้**ปากกา**กับ**ดินสอเขียนลงในสมุด**แล้ว
3. เอา**หนังสือ**มาจาก**กระเป๋าเป๋**ของฉันหน่อยได้ไหม?
4. ได้สิ ใน**ห้องเรียน**นี้หรือเปล่า?
5. ใช่ค่ะ อยู่ใน**กระเป๋าเป๋**ที่โต๊ะของฉัน
6. **ครู/อาจารย์**บอกว่าเราต้องทำ**ข้อสอบ**วันไหน?
7. วันพรุ่งนี้ครับ และ**นักเรียน/เด็กศึกษา**ทุกคนต้องเตรียมตัวให้ดี
8. โอเคค่ะ ขอบคุณนะ
9. ไม่เป็นไรครับ

✤ In Thai, the verb does not change form based on the subject, so it stays the same whether talking about "I", "you", "he", "she", or "they".

1. wan nîi rao mī **kān bān** yeūa ȟim?
2. mī khâ tæ̀ chạn chî **pākkā** kàb **dins̄ō** khȟan long nı **smud** læw
3. ao **nạngs̄eū** mā càk **kràpèā pê** khǒng chạn ǹxy dị̀ mị?
4. dị̀ s̄ī nı **ȟxng rīan** nîi ȟrụ̄x bplào?
5. chî khâ yǔ nı **kràpèā pê** thị̀ tô ̂tx kǒng chạn
6. **khrū/ācār̀** bxk wâ rao t̂xng thả **kĥxs̄xb** wan nı?
7. wan phrung nîi khrạb læ **nạk rīan/dèk s̄eḳhs̄'ā** thuk khn t̂xng trīym taw ȟî dī
8. o khe khâ ḳhxbkhuṇ ná
9. mị̀ bpen rı khrạb

1. Do we have **a lot of homework** today?
2. Yes, but I've already written it down in my **notebook** using a **pen** and **pencil**.
3. Can you get my **book** from my **backpack** for me, please?
4. Sure, is it in this **classroom**?
5. Yes, it's in the **backpack** on my desk.
6. When did the **teacher** say we have to take the **exam**?
7. Tomorrow, and every **student** must prepare well.
8. Okay, thank you.
9. You're welcome.

✤ In Thailand, King Rama VI was not only a monarch but also a philosopher, poet, and playwright, significantly influencing Thai literature and education.

วันที่ 99: หลากหลาย 2

1. วันนี้เป็น**วันหยุด**เนอะ
2. ใช่ มี**เทศกาล**อะไรหรือเปล่า?
3. มี**การฉลองงานเลี้ยง**ใหญ่ๆ ที่หมู่บ้านของฉัน
4. จะมี**เพลง**และ**การเต้นรำ**ด้วยหรือเปล่า?
5. แน่นอน แล้วยัง**มีของขวัญ**สำหรับทุกคนด้วย
6. ฟังดูสนุกมาก เราควร**จอง**วันนี้ไว้เลย
7. ใช่ มันเป็น**ประเพณี**ที่ดีที่เราควรรักษาไว้
8. ฉันจะไม่ลืมเอา**กุญแจ**บ้านมาด้วย
9. ดีมาก พบกันที่งานเลี้ยงนะ

✤ In Thai, the basic sentence structure follows the Subject-Verb-Object order, just like in English.

1. wan nî pen **wan hyut** neừ
2. chî mī **thētkān** xarị hreừ plào?
3. mī **kān chalǭng ngān lîang** yài yài thî mû bān khǒng chan
4. cà mī **phlēng** læ **kān tên ram** dūay hreừ plào?
5. næ̀nǭn læa yang mī **khǒng khwạn** sǎphạb thuk khon dūay
6. fang dū sǎnuk māk rao khwān **jǭng** wan nî wāi leo
7. chî man pen **praphēnî** thî dī thî rao khwān rakṣ'ā wāi
8. chan cà mị lūm ao **kun chæ** bān mā dūay
9. dī māk phob kan thī **ngān lîang** ná

DAY 99: MISCELLANEOUS II 🥄

1. Today is a **holiday**, isn't it?
2. Yes, is there any **festival** or something?
3. There's a big **celebration party** in my village.
4. Will there be **music** and **dancing** too?
5. Of course, and there will also be **gifts** for everyone.
6. Sounds like a lot of fun. We should **book** today off.
7. Yes, it's a good **tradition** that we should keep.
8. I won't forget to bring my **house keys**.
9. Great, see you at the **party**.

✤ In Thailand, it's common to celebrate a person's birthday at midnight by splashing them with water, symbolizing a refreshing start to their new year.

วันที่ ๑๐๐ : ขอแสดงความยินดีที่คุณได้ทำการเรียนจบ คู่มือแล้ว 🖋

1. สวัสดี! ฉันได้ยินว่าคุณเรียนจบแล้ว ขอแสดงความยินดีด้วยนะ
2. คุณมีแผนจะฉลองยังไงบ้าง?
3. ฉันคิดว่าเราควรจัดงานเลี้ยงเล็กๆ ที่บ้านของฉัน
4. ฉันจะทำกาแฟให้ และเราสามารถฟังเพลง นั่งเก้าอี้ คุยกันผ่านหน้าต่าง
5. และฉันมีของขวัญพิเศษให้คุณด้วย
6. มันเป็นหนังสือที่ฉันคิดว่าคุณจะชอบมาก
7. หลังจากนั้น เราสามารถไปขับรถยนต์ไปรอบๆ เพื่อฉลอง
8. อย่าลืมนำโทรศัพท์และคอมพิวเตอร์ของคุณมาด้วยนะ เผื่อเราต้องการค้นหา สถานที่ใหม่ๆ
9. ฉันหวังว่าคุณจะชอบการฉลองนี้!

✤ In Thai, to express congratulations, we often use the phrase "ขอแสดงความยินดี" followed by the reason for congratulations, ensuring the sentence reflects the completed action with appropriate verb tenses.

1. sawatdī! chaṇ dāi yin wā khun rīen cop lǣo khǭ s̄dæng khwām yindī dūay ná
2. khun mī phæn cà chalǭng yang ngai bāng?
3. chaṇ khid wā rao khūan cad ngān līeng lek̂ lek̂ thī̂ bān khǭng chaṇ
4. chaṇ cà tham kāfæ h̄ı̂ lǣa rao s̄āmārt fang phleng nâng kê̂ā xī̂ khuy kan phān ṅ̂ā tǎng
5. lǣa chaṇ mī khǭng khwǎn phis̄eṣ̄' h̄ı̂ khun dūay
6. man pen nǎngs̄ı̄ thī̂ chaṇ khid wā khun cà chǭb māk
7. h̄lạng cāk nán rao s̄āmārt pai khạb rth ynt pai rxb rxb pheụ̀x chalǭng
8. yà læum nam thōrās̄ạph lǣa khxmphiwtǒr khǭng khun mā dūay ná pheụ̀x rao t̂xngkār khīn h̄ạw thī̂ m̄ı̂
9. chaṇ h̄wạng wā khun cà chǭb kār chalǭng nī̂!

DAY 100: CONGRATULATIONS ON COMPLETING THE MANUAL 🍴

1. Hello! I heard you've graduated, congratulations!
2. Do you have any plans on how to celebrate?
3. I think we should have a small party at my place.
4. I'll make coffee, and we can listen to music, sit around, and chat through the window.
5. And I have a special gift for you too.
6. It's a book that I think you'll really like.
7. After that, we can go for a drive around to celebrate.
8. Don't forget to bring your phone and computer, just in case we want to look up new places.
9. I hope you'll enjoy this celebration!

♣ In Thailand, achieving success is often celebrated with a traditional Thai ceremony called "Khan Maak," where families and friends come together to share joy and blessings.

CHALLENGE NO. 10

PREPARE AND GIVE AN ORAL PRESENTATION IN THAI ON A TOPIC YOU ARE PASSIONATE ABOUT AND RECORD YOURSELF.

การเรียนรู้วัฒนธรรมใหม่เปิดประตูสู่โลกกว้าง

Learning new cultures opens the door to the wider world.

CONGRATULATIONS AND NEXT STEPS

CONGRATULATIONS

Congratulations on completing the 100 days of learning Thai! Your determination and perseverance have led you to succeed in this linguistic adventure.

You are now immersed in Thai and have acquired a solid vocabulary base, enabling you to understand and communicate in most everyday situations. This is a remarkable achievement in such a short time!

Throughout the lessons, you have developed mental mechanisms that encourage spontaneous understanding and natural conversation in Thai.

Be proud of yourself. You have achieved a level of autonomy that fully opens up the doors to the language and culture of Thailand.

. . .

The adventure continues! To maintain and refine your skills in Thai:

- Practice translating texts from English to Thai.
- Listen to our audios on shuffle to strengthen and refresh your vocabulary.
- Immerse yourself in the language: watch Thai dramas and listen to Thai music.
- If you're using Flashcards, continue their daily use.
- Communicate in Thai, with native speakers or via AI.

Congratulations again on this achievement! And see you soon in your continuous learning journey. สวัสดีครับ/ค่ะ (farewell word in the language)

WHAT'S NEXT?

Your success is undeniable, and to maintain your skills, continuous practice is essential.

Here are some ideas to continue progressing:

1. Review the vocabulary from this manual with our Flashcards.
2. Elevate your skills to a new level by discovering our intermediate-level manual or by exploring other NaturaLingua resources.
3. Join our online community: share, learn, and inspire others. Your journey can enlighten new learners.
4. Watch our video training and discover the secrets to mastering a language in just 100 days.
5. Fully immerse yourself in the language to reach new heights.

6. If you're ready for a new challenge, why not start a new language with our "Learn a Language in 100 Days" collection?

Learning a language is an endless adventure. Whether you deepen your knowledge of this language or embark on a new linguistic journey, the voyage never ends.

Congratulations and good luck on your continued journey!

ADDITIONAL RESOURCES

DOWNLOAD THE RESOURCES ASSOCIATED WITH THIS MANUAL AND GREATLY ENHANCE YOUR CHANCES OF SUCCESS.

Scan this QR code to access them:

SCAN ME

☞ **https://www.natura-lingua.com/download**

• **Optimize your learning with audio:** To significantly improve your language skills, we strongly advise you to download the audio files accompanying this manual. This will enhance your listening comprehension and pronunciation.

- **Enhance your learning with flashcards:** Flashcards are excellent tools for vocabulary memorization. We highly encourage you to use them to maximize your results. Download our set of cards, specially designed for this manual.

- **Join our learning community:** If you're looking to connect with other language enthusiasts through "Natura Lingua", we invite you to join our online group. In this community, you'll have the opportunity to ask questions, find learning partners, and share your progress.

- **Explore more with other Natura Lingua manuals:** If you like this method, note that there are other similar manuals for different languages. Discover our complete collection of manuals to enrich your linguistic learning experience in a natural and progressive way.

We are here to support you in learning the target language. For optimal results, we highly recommend downloading the audio and using the flashcards. These additional resources are designed to further facilitate your journey.

Happy learning!

ABOUT THE AUTHOR

 François Trésorier is a passionate polyglot and an expert in accelerated learning. He has developed unique learning methods that have helped over 31,400 people in more than 94 countries quickly achieve their learning goals.

With more than 7 years of research, testing, and developing innovative approaches for rapid language learning, he created the Natura Lingua method. This intuitive and natural method, based on the latest findings in cognition, enables quick language results.

When he's not creating new language learning manuals or helping his community achieve language results, François is involved in humanitarian efforts in the south and east of Ukraine.

Discover how the Natura Lingua method can transform your language learning.

Visit our website www.natura-lingua.com and join our dynamic community of passionate learners.

SHARE YOUR EXPERIENCE

Help Us Revolutionize Language Learning

I hope you found this manual enriching and useful. Our goal is to democratize this innovative and natural approach to language learning, to help as many people as possible quickly and easily achieve their linguistic goals. Your support is crucial for us. If you enjoyed this manual, we would be deeply grateful if you could take a moment to leave a review on Amazon KDP. Your feedback is not only a source of encouragement for us but also helps other language learners discover this method. Thank you immensely for your contribution to our project and best wishes on your language learning journey!

BY THE SAME AUTHOR

FIND ALL OUR NATURALINGUA BOOKS ON OUR WEBSITE

SCAN ME

We regularly add new titles to our collection. Feel free to visit our website to discover the latest releases:

http://www.natura-lingua.com/

This list is not exhaustive:

- English in 100 Days
- Spanish in 100 Days
- German in 100 Days
- Italian in 100 Days
- Portuguese in 100 Days
- Dutch in 100 Days
- Arabic in 100 Days
- Russian in 100 Days
- Chinese in 100 Days
- Japanese in 100 Days
- Korean in 100 Days

ESSENTIAL GLOSSARY

INDISPENSABLE WORDS AND THEIR
MEANINGS

Above - เหนือ

Actor/Actress - นักแสดง

Afternoon - บ่าย

Airplane - เครื่องบิน

Airport - สนามบิน

Allergy - แพ้

Alone - เหงา

Alone - เดียวดาย

Ambulance - รถพยาบาล

And - และ

And you? - คุณล่ะ?

Angry - โกรธ

Animal - สัตว์

Anxious - วิตกกังวล

Apartment - อพาร์ตเมนต์

App - แอปพลิเคชัน

Appetizer - โซฟา

Appetizer - อาหารเรียกน้ำย่อย

Application - แอปพลิเคชัน

April - เมษายน

Arm - แขน

Arrival - ถึง

Assistant - ช่วยเหลือ

ATM - เอทีเอ็ม

ATM - เครื่องเบิกเงินอัตโนมัติ

August - สิงหาคม

Aunt - ป้า หรือ น้า ขึ้นอยู่กับ
ว่าเป็นพี่หรือน้องของพ่อแม่

Aunt - ป้า หรือ น้า (en
fonction de la relation
familiale)

Author - นักเขียน

Autumn - ฤดูใบไม้ร่วง

Autumn - ใบไม้ร่วง

Back - หลัง

Backpack - กระเป๋าเป้

Bad - ไม่ดี

Baked - อบ

Balcony - ระเบียง

Band - วงดนตรี

Bank - ธนาคาร

Banknote - ธนบัตร

Bar - บาร์

Basket - ตะกร้า

Bathroom - ห้องน้ำ

Beach - หาดทราย

Bed - เตียง

Beef - เนื้อวัว

Beer - เบียร์

Behind - ข้างหลัง

Beside - ข้างๆ

Between - ระหว่าง

Bicycle - จักรยาน

Big - ใหญ่

Bike - จักรยาน

Bird - นก

Black - ดำ

Blog - บล็อก	Blue - น้ำเงิน	Boarding pass - บัตรโดยสาร
Boat - เรือ	Book - หนังสือ	Boss - เจ้านาย
Brain - สมอง	Bread - ขนมปัง	Brother - พี่ชาย / น้องชาย (selon l'âge relatif)
Brown - น้ำตาล	Browser - เบราว์เซอร์	Bus - รถบัส
Butter - เนย	Buy - ซื้อ	Cake - เค้ก
Calendar - ปฏิทิน	Calm - สงบ	Camera - กล้องถ่ายรูป
Canyon - หุบเขา	Car - รถยนต์	Cart - รถเข็น
Cash - เงินสด	Cashier - แคชเชียร์	Casual - สบายๆ
Cat - แมว	Cave - ถ้ำ	Ceiling - เพดาน
Celebration - การฉลอง	Centimeter - เซนติเมตร	Chair - เก้าอี้
Channel - ช่อง	Cheap - ถูก	Checkout - เคาน์เตอร์
Checkout - เคาน์เตอร์จ่ายเงิน	Cheese - ชีส	Chef - เชฟ
Chest - หน้าอก	Chicken - ไก่	Children - ลูกๆ
Chocolate - ช็อกโกแลต	Chocolate : Chocolate - ช็อคโกแลต : ช็อคโกแลต	Cinema - ภาพยนตร์
Classroom - ห้องเรียน	Climate - อากาศ	Clinic - คลินิก
Clock - นาฬิกา	Close - ใกล้	Clothes - เสื้อผ้า
Cloud - เมฆ	Coffee - กาแฟ	Coin - เหรียญ
Cold - เย็น	Colleague - เพื่อนร่วมงาน	Computer - คอมพิวเตอร์

Concert - คอนเสิร์ต	Conference - การประชุม	Confused - สับสน
Content - พอใจ	Continent - ทวีป	Cough - ไอ
Courtyard - ลาน	Cousin - ลูกพี่ลูกน้อง	Cow - วัว
Credit card - บัตรเครดิต	Culture - วัฒนธรรม	Currency - สกุลเงิน
Dance - การเต้น	Dance - การเต้นรำ	Danger - อันตราย
Day - วัน	Deadline - กำหนดส่ง	Debit card - บัตรเดบิต
December - ธันวาคม	Delayed - ล่าช้า	Delighted - ปลื้มปีติ
Dentist - ทันตแพทย์	Departure - ออกเดินทาง	Desert - ทะเลทราย
Dessert - ของหวาน	Discount - ส่วนลด	Doctor - แพทย์
Doctor - หมอ	Doctor - แพทย์	Dog - หมา
Door - ประตู	Down - ล่าง	Download - ดาวน์โหลด
Drawing - วาดรูป	Drink - เครื่องดื่ม	Drink - ดื่ม
Drizzle - ฝนปรอยๆ	Dry - แห้ง	Ear - หู
Earrings - ต่างหู	Earthquake - แผ่นดินไหว	Egg - ไข่
Eight - แปด	Eighteen - สิบแปด	Eleven - สิบเอ็ด
Email - อีเมล	Embassy - สถานทูต	Emergency - ฉุกเฉิน
Employee - พนักงาน	Evening - เย็น	Exam - การสอบ
Exam - ข้อสอบ	Exchange rate - อัตราแลกเปลี่ยน	Excited - ตื่นเต้น

Excuse me - ขอโทษครับ/ค่ะ (ครับ pour les hommes, ค่ะ pour les femmes)

Expensive - แพง

Eye - ตา

Face - หน้า

Family - ครอบครัว

Far - ไกล

Fast - เร็ว

Father - พ่อ

February - กุมภาพันธ์

Festival - เทศกาล

Fever - ไข้

Fiancé/Fiancée - คู่หมั้น

Fiction - นิยาย

Fifteen - สิบห้า

Finger - นิ้วมือ

Finger - นิ้ว

Fire - ไฟ

Fire - ไฟ

First aid - การปฐมพยาบาล

Fish - ปลา

Fitting room - ห้องลองเสื้อผ้า

Five - ห้า

Floor - พื้น

Flower - ดอกไม้

Foot - เท้า

Forecast - พยากรณ์

Forest - ป่า

Fork - ส้อม

Forty - สี่สิบ

Four - สี่

Fourteen - สิบสี่

Freezer - ตู้แช่แข็ง

Friday - วันศุกร์

Fried - ทอด

Friend - เพื่อน

Friends - เพื่อน

Fruit - ผลไม้

Fruits - ผลไม้

Full - เต็ม

Garage - โรงรถ

Garden - สวน

Gate - ประตู

Gift - ของขวัญ

Goat - แพะ

Gold - ทอง

Good - ดี

Good afternoon - สวัสดีตอนบ่าย

Good evening - สวัสดีตอนเย็น

Good night - ราตรีสวัสดิ์

Goodbye - ลาก่อน

Granddaughter - หลานสาว

Grandparents - ย่า / ยาย (pour la grand-mère) et ตา / ปู่ (pour le grand-père)

Grandson - หลานชาย

Grass - หญ้า

Green - เขียว	Grey - เทา	Grilled - ย่าง
Grocery store - ร้านขายของชำ	Guide - ไกด์	Hair - ผม
Hand - มือ	Happy - สุขใจ	Happy - ดีใจ
Hard - แข็ง	Hat - หมวก	Have a good day - ขอให้มีวันที่ดี
Head - หัว	Headache - ปวดหัว	Heavy - หนัก
Height - ความสูง	Hello - สวัสดี	Here - ที่นี่
Hi - สวัสดี	Hiking - เดินป่า	History - ประวัติศาสตร์
Holiday - วันหยุด	Homework - การบ้าน	Horse - ม้า
Hospital - โรงพยาบาล	Hospital - โรงพยาบาล	Hot - ร้อน
Hotel – โรงแรม	Hour - ชั่วโมง	House - บ้าน
How are you? - คุณสบายดีไหม?	How much does it cost? - ราคาเท่าไหร่	How much? - เท่าไหร่
How old are you? - คุณอายุเท่าไหร่?	How? - อย่างไร	Humid - ชื้น
Hurricane - พายุเฮอริเคน	Husband - สามี	I am - ฉันคือ
I am [age] years old - ฉันอายุ [อายุ] ปี	I am a [profession] - ฉันเป็น [อาชีพ]	I am fine - ฉันสบายดี
I am from [city/country] - ฉันมาจาก[เมือง/ประเทศ]	I am going - ฉันจะไป	I buy - ฉันซื้อ
I can - ฉันสามารถ	I give - ฉันให้	I have - ฉันมี
I know - ฉันรู้	I like music and sports - ฉันชอบดนตรีและกีฬา	I live in [city/country] - ฉันอยู่ที่[เมือง/ประเทศ]
I love you - ฉันรักคุณ	I miss you - ฉันคิดถึงคุณ	I need - ฉันต้องการ

I understand - เข้าใจ	I watch - ฉันดู	I would like - ฉันอยากได้
I'm joking - ฉันล้อเล่น	Ice cream - ไอศกรีม	Ice-cream : Ice Cream - ไอศกรีม : ไอศกรีม
In - ใน	Inch - นิ้ว	Indigenous - ชาวพื้นเมือง
Injury - บาดแผล	Inn - ที่พัก	Inside - ข้างใน
Internet - อินเทอร์เน็ต	Island - เกาะ	Jacket - เสื้อแจ็คเก็ต
Jam - แยม	January - มกราคม	Jewelry - เครื่องประดับ
Job - การจ้างงาน	Joyful - ร่าเริง	Juice - น้ำผลไม้
Juice : Juice - น้ำผลไม้ : น้ำผลไม้	July - กรกฎาคม	June - มิถุนายน
Jungle - ดงดิบ	Jungle - ป่าดงดิบ	Jungle - ป่าดิบชื้น
Key - กุญแจ	Kilogram - กิโลกรัม	Kitchen - ห้องครัว
Knee - เข่า	Knife - มีด	Lake - ทะเลสาบ
Lamp - โคมไฟ	Laptop - แล็ปท็อป	Large - ใหญ่
Lawyer - ทนายความ	Leaf - ใบไม้	Left - ซ้าย
Leg - ขา	Length - ความยาว	Lesson - บทเรียน
Light - เบา	Lightning - ฟ้าผ่า	Liquid - ของเหลว
Living room - ห้องนั่งเล่น	Lock - ล็อค	Long - ยาว
Look - ดู	Loud - ดัง	Low - ต่ำ
Luggage - สัมภาระ	Luggage - กระเป๋าเดินทาง	Main course - อาหารจานหลัก

Man - ชาย	Manager - ผู้จัดการ	Map - แผนที่
March - มีนาคม	Market - ตลาด	May - พฤษภาคม
Maybe - อาจจะ	Meat - เนื้อสัตว์	Medicine - ยา
Meeting - การประชุม	Menu - เมนู	Meter - เมตร
Midnight - เที่ยงคืน	Milk - นม	Milk : Milk - นม : นม
Minute - นาที	Monday - วันจันทร์	Month - เดือน
Morning - เช้า	Mother - แม่	Mountain - ภูเขา
Mouse - หนู	Mouth - ปาก	Movie - ภาพยนตร์
Museum - พิพิธภัณฑ์	Music - เพลง	Music - ดนตรี
My name is... - ฉันชื่อ...	Near - ใกล้	Neck - คอ
Necklace - สร้อยคอ	Neighbor - เพื่อนบ้าน	Nephew - หลานชาย
Nervous - กระวนกระวาย	New - ใหม่	News - ข่าว
Nice to meet you! - ยินดีที่ได้พบคุณ	Niece - หลานสาว	Night - คืน
Nine - เก้า	Nineteen - สิบเก้า	No - ไม่
Non-fiction - หนังสือเชิงสารคดี	Noon - เที่ยง	Nose - จมูก
Notebook - สมุด	Novel - นวนิยาย	November - พฤศจิกายน
Now - ตอนนี้	Ocean - มหาสมุทร	October - ตุลาคม
Office - สำนักงาน	Okay - ตกลง	Old - เก่า

On the left - ทางซ้าย	On the right - ทางขวา	One - หนึ่ง
Online - ออนไลน์	Orange - ส้ม	Oven - เตาอบ
Over there - ที่นั่น	Painting - จิตรกรรม	Pan - กระทะ
Parents - พ่อแม่	Park - สวนสาธารณะ	Partner - หุ้นส่วน
Partner - คู่ค้า หรือ แฟน (en fonction du contexte)	Partner - คู่ค้า	Party - งานเลี้ยง
Passport - หนังสือเดินทาง	Password - รหัสผ่าน	Pasta - พาสต้า
Pastry : Pastry - ขนมอบ : ขนมอบ	Pen - ปากกา	Pencil - ดินสอ
Pepper - พริกไทย	Pharmacy - ร้านขายยา	Photography - การถ่ายภาพ
Pie : Pie - พาย : พาย	Pig - หมู	Pill - เม็ดยา
Pink - ชมพู	Plane - เครื่องบิน	Plant - พืช
Plate - จาน	Play - เล่น	Play - ละคร
Please - กรุณา	Poetry - กวีนิพนธ์	Police - ตำรวจ
Police - ตำรวจ	Pond - บึง	Pork - หมู
Port - ท่าเรือ	Prescription - ใบสั่งยา	Presentation - การนำเสนอ
President - ประธาน	Price - ราคา	Printer - เครื่องพิมพ์
Proud - ภูมิใจ	Radio - วิทยุ	Railway station - สถานีรถไฟ
Rain - ฝน	Rainbow - รุ้ง	Reading - การอ่าน
Receipt - ใบเสร็จ	Red - แดง	Refrigerator - ตู้เย็น

Refund - การคืนเงิน	Relative - ญาติ	Relaxed - ผ่อนคลาย
Remote control - รีโมท	Remote control - รีโมท คอนโทรล	Report - รายงาน
Reservation - การจอง	Restaurant - ร้านอาหาร	Rice - ข้าว
Right - ขวา	River - แม่น้ำ	Roasted - ย่าง
Roof - หลังคา	Room - ห้อง	Room - ห้องนอน
Round - กลม	Sad - เศร้า	Safe - ปลอดภัย
Salad - สลัด	Sale - ลดราคา	Sandwich - แซนด์วิช
Saturday - วันเสาร์	Saucepan - หม้อ	Scared - กลัว
Schedule - ตารางเวลา	School - โรงเรียน	Screen - หน้าจอ
Sea - ทะเล	Second - วินาที	See you later - เจอกันใหม่
Sell - ขาย	September - กันยายน	Seven - เจ็ด
Seventeen - สิบเจ็ด	Shape - รูปร่าง	Sheep - แกะ
Ship - เรือ	Ship - เรือใหญ่	Shirt - เสื้อ
Shoes - รองเท้า	Shopping centre - ศูนย์การค้า	Shopping mall - ศูนย์การค้า
Shoulder - ไหล่	Singer - นักร้อง	Singing - การร้องเพลง
Sister - พี่สาว / น้องสาว (selon l'âge relatif)	Six - หก	Sixteen - สิบหก
Size - ขนาด	Skiing - สกี	Skin - ผิวหนัง
Skirt - กระโปรง	Slow - ช้า	Small - เล็ก

Smartphone - สมาร์ทโฟน	Snowboarding - สโนว์บอร์ด	Snowflake - [หิมะ]
Social media - โซเชียลเน็ตเวิร์ก	Social media - โซเชียลมีเดีย	Soda - โซดา
Soda : Soft Drink - โซดา : โซดา	Soft - นุ่ม	Song - เพลง
Sorry - เสียใจ	Soup - ซุป	South - แน
Spoon - ช้อน	Spring - ฤดูใบไม้ผลิ	Spring - [ฤดูใบไม้ผลิ]
Square - สี่เหลี่ยม	Stairs - บันได	Station - สถานีรถไฟ
Stop - หยุด	Stop here - หยุดที่นี่	Store - ร้านค้า
Storm - พายุ	Straight ahead - ตรงไป	Stream - ลำธาร
Stressed - เครียด	Student - นักเรียน	Student - นักเรียน/เด็กศึกษา
Subject - วิชา	Subway - รถไฟฟ้าใต้ดิน	Suitcase - กระเป๋าเดินทาง
Summer - ฤดูร้อน	Summer - ร้อน	Sunday - วันอาทิตย์
Sunglasses - แว่นตากันแดด	Sunshine - แดด	Sunshine - แดดจ้า
Supermarket - ซูเปอร์มาร์เก็ต	Swimming - ว่ายน้ำ	Table - โต๊ะ
Tall - สูง	Taxi - แท็กซี่	Tea - ชา
Teacher - ครู	Teacher - ครู/อาจารย์	Telephone - โทรศัพท์
Television - โทรทัศน์	Ten - สิบ	Terminal - อาคารผู้โดยสาร
Thank you - ขอบคุณ	thank you! - ขอบคุณ!	That way - ทางนั้น
The day after tomorrow - มะรืนนี้	Theater - โรงละคร	There - ที่นั่น

Thirteen - สิบสาม	Thirty - สามสิบ	Thirty-Eight - สามสิบแปด
Thirty-Five - สามสิบห้า	Thirty-Four - สามสิบสี่	Thirty-Nine - สามสิบเก้า
Thirty-One - สามสิบเอ็ด	Thirty-Seven - สามสิบเจ็ด	Thirty-Six - สามสิบหก
Thirty-Three - สามสิบสาม	Thirty-Two - สามสิบสอง	This way - ทางนี้
Three - สาม	Thrilled - ปลื้ม	Thunder - เสียงฟ้าร้อง
Thunder - ฟ้าร้อง	Thursday - วันพฤหัสบดี	Ticket - ตั๋ว
Time - เวลา	Toast - ขนมปังปิ้ง	Toast : Toast - โทสต์ : โทสต์
Toaster - เครื่องปิ้งขนมปัง	Today - วันนี้	Tomorrow - พรุ่งนี้
Tooth - ฟัน	Toothache - ปวดฟัน	Tornado - พายุทอร์นาโด
Tourist - นักท่องเที่ยว	Tradition - ประเพณี	Train - รถไฟ
Tram - รถราง	Tree - ต้นไม้	Trolley - รถเข็น
Trousers - กางเกง	Truck - รถบรรทุก	Tuesday - วันอังคาร
Tuesday, - วันอังคาร,	Turn - เลี้ยว	Turn left - เลี้ยวซ้าย
Turn right - เลี้ยวขวา	Twelve - สิบสอง	Twenty - ยี่สิบ
Twenty-Eight - ยี่สิบแปด	Twenty-Five - ยี่สิบห้า	Twenty-Four - ยี่สิบสี่
Twenty-Nine - ยี่สิบเก้า	Twenty-One - ยี่สิบเอ็ด	Twenty-Seven - ยี่สิบเจ็ด
Twenty-Six - ยี่สิบหก	Twenty-Three - ยี่สิบสาม	Twenty-Two - ยี่สิบสอง
Two - สอง	Uncle - ลุง หรือ น้า ขึ้นอยู่กับ ว่าเป็นพี่หรือน้องของพ่อแม่	Uncle - ลุง หรือ น้า (en fonction de la relation familiale)

Under - ใต้	University - มหาวิทยาลัย	Up - บน
Upset - ไม่พอใจ	Upset - หงุดหงิด	Username - ชื่อผู้ใช้
Valley - หุบเขา	Vegetables - ผัก	Visa - วีซ่า
Volcano - ภูเขาไฟ	Waiter/Waitress - พนักงานเสิร์ฟ	Wall - ผนัง
Warm - ร้อน	Water - น้ำ	Water : Water - น้ำ : น้ำ
Website - เว็บไซต์	Wednesday - วันพุธ	Week - สัปดาห์
Weekend - สุดสัปดาห์	Weight - น้ำหนัก	Wet - เปียก
What day is it today? - วันนี้วันอะไร?	What do you do for a living? - คุณทำอะไร	What do you like? - คุณชอบอะไร
What is your name? - คุณชื่ออะไร?	What time is it? - กี่โมงแล้ว	What? - อะไร
When? - เมื่อไหร่	Where are you from? - คุณมาจากที่ไหน	Where do you live? - คุณอยู่ที่ไหน
Where? - ไหน	Which one? - ไหน	White - ขาว
Who? - ใคร	Why? - ทำไม	Wi-Fi - ไวไฟ
Wide - กว้าง	Width - ความกว้าง	Wife - ภรรยา
Window - หน้าต่าง	Wine - ไวน์	Wine : Wine - ไวน์ : ไวน์
Winter - หนาว	Woman - หญิง	Worried - กังวล
Year - ปี	Yellow - เหลือง	Yes - ใช่
Yesterday - เมื่อวาน	You're welcome - ไม่เป็นไร	Youth hostel - ที่พักแบบหอพัก

Made in the USA
Columbia, SC
18 September 2024

42532050R00170